Wings of Destiny

Wings of Destiny

*How Learning To Let Go Can
Release Your Inner Power
And Be The Key To Your
Success*

Corinna Stringer

Wings of Destiny
How Learning To Let Go Can Release Your Inner Power And Be The Key To Your Success
© 2023 Corinna Stringer

ISBN: 9798367032659 Paperback

Published by: Bestselling Book Publishing
Cover Designed By: Tanya Grant – The TNG Designs Group Limited

The strategies in this book are presented primarily for enjoyment and educational purposes. Every effort has been made to trace copyright holders and obtain their permission for the use of copyright material.

The information and resources provided in this book are based upon the authors' personal experiences. Any outcome, income statements or other results, are based on the authors' experiences and there is no guarantee that your experience will be the same. There is an inherent risk in any business enterprise or activity and there is no guarantee that you will have similar results as the author as a result of reading this book.

The author reserves the right to make changes and assumes no responsibility or liability whatsoever on behalf of any purchaser or reader of these materials.

Acknowledgement

Firstly, I would like to say how eternally grateful I am to *my loving grandparents*. Who raised me, supported me, taught me so much, helped me financially and emotionally. You will always & forever be in my heart and part of every success achieve.

To my dear friends *Steven* and *Kerry* who have supported me and always been there for me and my family.

My two beautiful cats *Skyela* and *Gizzy*, yes I know what you are thinking... but, when you have severe depression yet you have 2 pawfect reasons to get up in the morning. They have truly saved my life.

Jessen James for not only being my amazingly heart led business and speaker mentor but also becoming a great friend.

Kevin McDonnell, thank you for being a brilliant property mentor, for giving me the support, guidance and words of advice when I needed them.

And to my new found family!

My community far too many to name here, you know who you are….

The wonderfully supportive people who I have met throughout my entrepreneurial journey. We have worked together, crewed together, laughed and cried together.

"Family isn't always blood. It's the people in your life who want you in theirs; the ones who accept you for who you are. The ones who would do anything to see to smile and succeed and who love you no matter what"

My Mum for teaching me how not to be in life! Which lead me to be the loving, caring person I am today. Without this type of upbringing maybe I would have had no need to go on a journey of discovery, becoming more understanding with others and most importantly, learned the art of forgiveness.

My *haters* who drove me, my *abusers* who strengthened me, my *doubters* who pushed me… for this I thank you all…

Foreword

Life has a funny way of beating you down when you least expect it. Along our journey of living this interesting life, we often find ourselves in situations where either people, circumstances or ourselves let us down. The challenge with this is that it often carries emotional wounds. These emotional wounds then start to manifest in other areas of life, such as, our health, relationships, careers and finances. If we don't do something functional about this, we will never ever live the lives we truly deserve.

You see, it is my belief that we get one life, and you must live it. In order to live it, we must put to bed the things that hold us back, otherwise we cannot fly to new heights.

I have had the pleasure of training tens of thousands of people across the world. Every now and then throughout my travels I get to meet and work with some incredible people. One of those incredible people is the author of this book, Corinna Stringer. I have known her for many years and one thing I have learned from Corinna is to never ever give up.

She has a tenacity and drive to see things through, even when they don't work out in the way she wants them to and somehow finds a way to keep on going and get to where she wants to go. She has put all the lessons from her life journey, her trials and tribulations, her setbacks and her come backs in this book so that you can finally start looking at what it is you need to do to let go of anything that is holding you back right now, so you, just like Corinna, can start flying.

I highly recommend that whilst reading this book, you not only take on board what Corinna is saying but that you also implement it. Read this book like your life depends on it and watch how you too can leave your past behind you so that you too can fly high just like an eagle.

Jessen James
Award Winning Speaker and CEO of Global Success Ltd

Dedication

I would like to dedicate this book to my Nan and Grandad.

To our wonderful community.

To all the loved ones in my life.

And to you... to your success, despite adversity and challenges you may experience past, present, or future. I know and trust in you to get through them and become the luminary self you truly are.

"Believe in your wings and fly"

TABLE OF CONTENTS

Introduction.. 1

Chapter 1 19

Chapter 2 33

Chapter 3 41

Chapter 4 57

Chapter 5 63

Chapter 6 73

Chapter 7 86

Chapter 8 99

Chapter 9 107

Chapter 10 112

Chapter 11 126

Chapter 12 138

Chapter 13 140

Chapter 14 154

My Lessons, My Learnings, and My Message to You
.... 164

About the Author 215

Introduction

What is Your Destiny?

We each have our own idea of what success is. Our own reasons as to why we think we cannot pursue a dream, or reach our destiny.

And, whether we like to acknowledge it or not, we also each have an 'inner voice' that will pop up at some time in our lives, encouraging us to procrastinate, instead of focusing on a goal.

The first dilemma we face in trying to *achieve* success, is understanding what it actually means to us, as an individual. To be able to turn that 'idea' of success into reality.

How will you know you've achieved success or been successful if you don't know what success means to you? What will success *look* like for you? What will it *feel* like? What will life *be* like when you *are* successful?

At this point, I will say, it takes more than simply reading a paragraph, or even a book, and asking a couple of questions. This is just your starting point, remember!

This next step also applies to you if you already know what your version of success is, and yet still haven't managed to achieve it. Or if you are one of the many thousands of business owners who have worked incredibly hard, achieved that magical six to seven figure turnover, yet seem to have hit a plateau and you're struggling to reach the next elusive milestone number.

So before you go any further, ask these questions of yourself.

- What are your "reasons" for not pursuing your dream?

- What has stopped you from reaching your destiny?

- Why have you been unable, so far, to achieve success?

This is fascinating if you are willing to open up to unravelling, by the way! Obviously, we're not going to go through the whole process in this introduction, it can take hours, weeks, months or longer.

As coaches and mentors, we often compare this element of inner work to peeling away the layers of an onion. You see, we don't realise how much is hidden away in the layers of our life experiences, until we try to understand what causes us to do things the way we do (or not to even try, as the case may be).

And there is definitely another connection to peeling an onion when doing the inner work, as tears are inevitable! Don't let this put you off though. I can hand on heart tell you that letting the tears flow freely whilst unpeeling the layers of your life is an intrinsic, and incredibly cathartic, part of the healing process.

It's when we start to look into these so-called "reasons" for not pursuing our dreams and fulfilling our destiny, that we discover they are actually *excuses*.

Each excuse comes from an experience we are reminded of, that our brain simply doesn't want us to go back to. A situation that has caused us hurt or discomfort, left us with a negative emotion, feeling like a failure, or that created heartache and pain.

The more we think about this situation (or situations), the less likely we are to want to go back to that place, time, or experience again.

Why would we want to feel that same hurt, embarrassment, or shame all over again?

And so, these excuses build up over time. They stop us from doing whatever it is that will help us succeed and reach our destiny. And as we have no control over them, until we know and understand what's going on, we believe they are genuine "reasons."

We tell ourselves over and over that we can't do certain things.

It's just not me. I don't do technology – never have, never will.

I couldn't possibly get on a stage and talk to people the way you do!

And, before we know it, we have talked ourselves out of everything! Our ideas of success remain just that. We never bring the pictures and words on our vision boards to life, or off the paper and spreadsheets where we've planned them all out.

Think about your own circumstances. What opportunities have you missed out on, simply by talking yourself out of it?

Where could you have been right now?

How could your business, your life, and your relationships be looking and feeling right now, had you not allowed your reasons (excuses) to step up and take centre stage, instead of you being up there yourself?

Of course, it doesn't have to be something as huge as literally being up there on a stage, or delivering a workshop, keynote speech, or writing a book!

Are you disappointed with yourself for not even taking the first step, and then the next tiny step forward?

Do you allow yourself to fall prey to the voices inside your head telling you not to do anything that will push you out of your comfort zone? The inner chatter, or 'mind monkeys', that keep you small and quiet for fear of falling into the same perceived danger, embarrassment, or criticism, that you experienced maybe even just once before. Do you wish you had made that first move in a personal or business connection?

We are our own worst enemy at times. We let ourselves down, become disheartened with ourselves, and then settle in a state of resentment because we've not met our goals and dreams.

The inner voices (mind monkeys or chimp mind) are astonishingly powerful, and far too complex to do justice in one paragraph. Professor Steve Peters refers to this as the Chimp Paradox, where the "chimp" mind tries to hijack the human logical mind.

Yes, there is an argument to say that what is meant to be yours will come to you if you put the inspired action in place. But you have to take that action. Whatever is meant to be yours does not come to you handed on a plate!

I can teach you to reframe any regrets you may have when you look back on missed opportunities. So by getting to grips with those things that you've let pass you by, and noting them down now, you're already gaining a head start to move you forward from here.

Success *can* be achieved. You *can* reach your destiny.

So, how do some people find themselves living their passion, and others only ever dream about it?

Well, I'm sure you can recall a time when you have heard someone say......

Opportunities don't happen to me
I don't have enough time
I don't have enough money
My family or friends never support me
What will people think?
People will think I'm trying to be someone I am not
What if I fail? They'll all say, "I told you so."
It is too hard
I don't know how
Where do I start?
Why me?

Have you caught your own inner voice saying at least one of the above?

If you are thinking to yourself right now,

"I don't have a little voice that controls what I do."

Well, I'm afraid to tell you, that's it right there!

And you're about to learn all about the little voices I've picked up through the years. The ones that have both stopped me from doing what I wanted to do, but also the ones that drove me forward.

Before that, just a little bit more technical information to explain what goes on inside our minds – literally, what goes on behind the scenes.

The Technical Part

Without us even knowing, our minds take on board around 12 million bits of information every day. To put this into context, a 64-gigabyte phone for instance, would be full in less than an hour!

So what happens with all these bits of information? Surely we cannot possibly retain and make use of it all?

Well, some go into our **unconscious mind**, because once we know how to do certain things, these things soon become actions we do without a second thought. Second nature. Like how to drive a car, ride a bike, or brush our teeth. They no longer need to sit at the front of our minds or in the forefront of our thoughts, however you like to explain it.

Others enter the **conscious mind**, and it seems we are constantly thinking those thoughts (these are at the front of our minds). Once we are consciously aware of something, it appears over and over.

Deepak Chopra states that some of our thoughts are so much at the forefront of our minds, we simply cannot get them out of our heads. So much so, that 95% of our thoughts are the same thoughts we thought yesterday!

Now that certainly is something to think about!

As for the rest? Well, they are deemed as 'not important enough' to process, or for our minds to do anything with. So they just fleetingly pass through.

Then, one of three things happens to the information that's brought into our awareness, based on the patterns the mind recognises from the past. It **distorts**, **deletes**, or **generalises**.

Of course, there is a much more technical explanation of the thought process, but we'll save that for another day and another time. If you are interested, I go into much more detail about it and include it within the NLP (Neuro Linguistic Programming) work in my coaching programmes.

For now, though, think your deliberate, guiding, and conscious thoughts are in control of your actions?

Think again ...

We retain information not just from what we *hear*, but also from what we *see*, and how things make us *feel*.

If something comes into our awareness often enough, it becomes the norm. Our brain thinks we want to do something with it, because we have paid attention to it when we've heard it, seen it, or felt it before. And so it gets dropped into our unconscious (subconscious) mind. The bike riding, cleaning teeth, etc.

For example, when we are surrounded by negativity and negative language at every turn, that is all we think about. Our own habits and behaviours change accordingly. We might start to speak negatively, and think negative thoughts about ourselves and others. That too, becomes second nature, the "norm". We do it without consciously trying.

Or, when we smell a scent on a friend, ex-partner, or someone we are frequently in close contact with, the next time we smell the same scent on a different person, we might find ourselves thinking of that first person. Chances are, we might also feel emotions towards that person too. Perhaps the emotions we felt when we were with that person, which could have been totally unrelated to them, but we simply recall how we felt when we caught their scent. Or it might be a reminder of how that person made us feel (positively or negatively).

Do you see why I'm trying to limit the technical explanations?!

Of course, certain thoughts are there to protect us.

These are the ones that I mentioned before. The ones that serve as a reminder of something that happened many years ago, generally in our childhood (as that is when the majority of our core beliefs develop), and will try to stop us from going back to that place or experience again.

These can form what we now know as "limiting beliefs." They might stop us from doing something like standing up in front of a room of colleagues to do a presentation. Or make a phone call, for personal or business purposes. Stop us from taking gym classes or doing something that we THINK we really want to do, but just can't seem to bring ourselves to do it.

In fact, we might not know how, why, or whether it is linked to our past, or why it's stopping us in our tracks now. All we know is, our mind tells us "It's a NO from me."

This is just one of the many elements of my client work that I love to see. The moments of realisation when we put the pieces together and they understand the connections between their past and their present behaviours are outstanding! They feel lighter, free, and ready to take on anything. It's like that missing piece of the jigsaw you've been searching for all this time!

So remember, we're all in this together. And I imagine just about every single one of you has experienced at least one of these blocks. Yes, I can feel the nods! If you're shaking your head right now, I will bet my hat on the fact it will happen at some time, and possibly already has, but you didn't (want to) notice it.

Did you also know that some of our thoughts and feelings have been adopted over time through what we call '*conditioning*'?

These are the learned thoughts and behaviours we pick up and collect from others as we grow up. The thoughts that have been passed onto us from our parents, grandparents, other family members, friends, and those we look up to or have been inspired by in some way.

These conditioned thoughts and beliefs, like I said, have likely been nurtured since before the age of seven. Some could have been collected pre-birth, in the womb, or during birth. Amazingly, whether you care to believe this or not, some could have even been from past lives.

The irony is, that as we reach a certain age, many of these conditioned thoughts, feelings, and behaviours are no longer serving us any purpose at all. It's just always been that way, so that's the way it is.

Sadly, as children, we do not have a choice. We are conditioned or guided by our family and other influential people around us.

Do you remember being told, "children should be seen, and not heard?" That's definitely an old favourite passed down through the generations. We were often reminded to speak only when spoken to. And never to question.

The thoughts and beliefs could relate to money and create a money mindset that we become stuck with, and have to work hard to really understand what we are gaining from retaining such beliefs. Only then, once we have processed old versus new beliefs, can we truly let go and move on.

Or, even as we enter the workplace in a learning or trainee role, we ask a colleague why something is done a certain way, and they tell us "it's just always been done that way."

As adults, though, we *do* have a choice.

A choice to let go of what we have learned, or how we have been primed to be, if it no longer serves us.

We have a choice to learn to love ourselves, and to believe in ourselves once again.

A choice to set our own goals, create our own destiny, and achieve our own version of success.
Whilst writing this book, I was thinking about what you, my readers, would like to learn.

I know when giving a gift or something of value, we like to make people happy or feel good. It is a natural human trait, and certainly something I have always aimed for.

True happiness is for you to find. This book is to help you discover some of the realisations to get you on your journey, and to discover your true power from within.

The reason for sharing my story is to tell you the truth.

Please remember, though, that this is *my* truth. An important point to make clear, as there are many versions of the truth - something else that children are often *not* taught to appreciate.

As children, we only see one dimension of the truth – that of our own truth.

In my case though, my version of the truth has helped me to become the person I am today. It has given me the resilience to battle on through some pretty tough times. And it is the reason I am here talking to you through whatever medium you have chosen to access my journey so far.

I will be telling you my story, what I have learned from life and the people who have been influential within my life, the techniques I have also learned over the years, and how I turned my pains into power to get me here.

Although I would not wish similar experiences on anyone (and I wouldn't necessarily recommend taking the same steps as I have done at times!) It fills me with a huge sense of gratitude and pride to know that, by the time you finish my story, you will be able to relate to at least some parts. And feel inspired enough to know that you, too, can overcome so much more than you might think.

Having the courage to share some of my own personal childhood accounts that destroyed my self-esteem, and the repeat pattern of self-destruction that was borne as a result will, I have no doubt, be triggering for some of you. And for that, I apologise in advance. Of course, that is not my intention.

However, if it were not for my learning and my personal growth, which I do genuinely want to share with you to help you through your tough times too, I would not have the confidence to do so.

You see, without going through inner work and reaching a heightened level of self-awareness, we continue through life's journey oblivious to anything different. We remain in that child-like unquestioning state.

And through self-awareness, we can start to reveal, process, and move on from experiences in our past that have caused us to doubt ourselves, hate ourselves, and generally hold us back.

Without self-belief, we fall into the trap of doubting ourselves over and over. We attract negativity, and the wrong people and events, into our lives. People who pull us down. People whom we believe are 'perfect' for us at the time, because we fail to comprehend how we can possibly deserve anything other than being in that situation, or receiving that treatment. And we are generally stopped from becoming the amazing, empowered beings we are meant to be.

They say that when you can tell your story, and it doesn't make you cry, then you have healed.

It takes time, effort, courage, and trust to reach that stage, considering how much torment, fear, and trauma life may have thrown at you.

However, may I just add that through a great personal transformation journey, which I proudly teach my clients today, I have learned to *Forgive, Rebuild, and Grow.*

"To forgive is to set a prisoner free and to discover that the prisoner was you" Lewis B. Smedes.

Throughout "Wings of Destiny", and the learnings I share with you, you will learn:

- ✔ How to change the outcome of your situation by thinking differently.
- ✔ How your own words, in your head and spoken, have a huge impact on your results in life.
- ✔ How I turned my own heartache and pain into *your* new power.
- ✔ How to feel happier and less stressed.
- ✔ How to live with passion and purpose every day.

This book *may not* be for you if:

- You have never experienced pain in your life
- You have all the success you have ever dreamed of, and
- You are living your life purposely, and truly fulfilled, every day.

If any of the above three points apply to you, please be kind enough to gift "Wings of Destiny" to someone you care for, so they may benefit and learn.

On that note, let's dive in, share the love, and I hope to give you all a chance to fulfil your own Destiny!!!!

My Story

Chapter 1

A Vision Through Someone Else's Window

Bullied for being ginger, ugly, shy, and not particularly smart, I didn't exactly have it easy!

I remember the first day I went to preschool. Incidentally, there were no first-day tears for me when I toddled off to meet the teacher. I had already learned to just get on with things by then. Once I was settled inside the classroom, I was told I could choose anything to play with, and try to mix with the other children. I found an amazing toy kitchen (you'll see the irony and relevance of this later) so there I was, happily playing with the brightly coloured pots, pans, and cleaning equipment, when two children came up to me and shoved me out of the way.

"No!" one of them shouted at me, as the other one stepped in front of me and pushed me backwards so I almost fell.

And just like that, I wasn't allowed to play with them.

Why would they do that? I didn't understand.

Feeling sad, sorry, and totally confused, I couldn't really see anything else I wanted to do, so I sat with the teacher all day. I felt safe there.

From that day, I would spend playtimes with the teacher or teaching assistant on duty, holding their hand or just following them around. I was like that proverbial little lost sheep. At lunch times, you would find me clinging to the dinner ladies, walking around the yard, making sure all the other children were happily playing, and staying out of trouble.

I didn't talk to the others though. I kept myself well away from them at every possible opportunity.

I never joined in with the little groups dotted around the school, singing or playing games. I didn't actually know *how* to behave around other children, which you'll also find out as I continue to walk you through my story.

In fact, throughout my entire school life, I didn't really interact much with the other children at all.

I never wanted to feel that same rejection in school again.

I felt enough of it at home.

Life for me back then was surreal.

I can't say I ever got to experience being a child in my own house. My grandparents treated me like a child. They bought me paddling pools, clothes, and toys. My grandad built me my first swing and monkey bar. I was so proud to tell people about it. And they let me be the kid I should have been.

I don't remember much of that with mum. Maybe a couple of dolls to dress up and make up little adventures, imaginary conversations, in an escape from reality, as little girls did. I think we had some games and a few puzzles, which kept me quiet. Mum liked that.

She would often host these parties at home. You know the ones where the house could have burst with the number of people in it. Many of whom I had never seen before, and then would very rarely see again either. She was fine with them wandering in and out of all our rooms. I thought it was a bit strange. But I did my job, took their coats when they arrived, and piled them nicely out of the way.

Our entire home always had a really strong smell of different perfumes and aftershaves for days and days after the party had finished.

My other 'job' was to serve drinks and canapes for her "friends" on trays. Mum thought she was the bee's knees gliding around the room with her cigarette in a posh silver holder, and being the centre of attention.

Even in my early years, I had to hold adult conversations. Mum used to pretend she was really proud of me, and show me off to her so-called friends. But as soon as she was done with me, I'd get told to go off to my room, and play quietly.

Pushed away to one side.

The thing I remember about starting school is that we always had huge expectations and a tingling excitement of making new friends, playing, and generally having fun. We would look forward to show and tell, and talking about what our families had been doing at the weekend or during the holidays.

There should be no sign of any fear of what might happen. No fear of what's to come. No fear of anything in fact. Just the expectation of meeting new friends, getting to play out in the playground or on the field in the summer. Just being children.

And yet, from day one, I remember the class being told to sit on the mat with our fingers over our mouths. We must listen. And not question. We were told what to do, rather than being guided, given clear instructions, and supported into becoming confident young people.

We knew no better at that age though, did we?

During infants, because of those selfish children in the toy kitchen on my first day at preschool, I kept quiet most of the time. I guess I didn't come across as the brightest kid. And I couldn't grasp things as quickly as some of the other children in my class, so not many of them wanted to be my friend anyway.

I would waste hours, fidgeting, sitting there worrying about things, and never making much progress.

And gradually, I started to avoid going to the teacher for help too.

One teacher in my primary school, I'll call her Miss H.... the thought of this now makes me laugh, and I actually passed her in my car a few years ago. It was a shame that I couldn't stop and tell her how so very wrong she had been about me, and how bad she'd made me feel about myself for so many years.

I remember one parents' evening when she was telling my mum and nan how "lazy" I was. Of course, my mum agreed with everything she said. She didn't want to kick up a fuss or cause a scene. Anything to stay on the right side of the teachers and not stand out in any way.

But my nan, the biggest and most vocal supporter in my life, didn't agree with the comments at all. She saw so much more in me than my mum ever did. That was just one of the many occasions I felt so awkwardly caught up between my mum and my beloved nan.

Anyway, back to the classroom, I eventually had to go to Miss H on this one particular day. I had to admit that I didn't understand the work we'd all been given. Nobody else would help me. Not that I expected they would have given me the right answer anyway. It was far too easy to take the mickey out of me. I was too easy to take advantage of.

For some reason, this time though, I decided to ask Miss H for help.

Instead of the reaction I thought I would get (I had hoped for some gentle words and a little bit more of an explanation at least), she snatched the workbook out of my tiny little hands, and dragged me by my arm to the corner of the room. She told me to sit on the mat. Practically shoving me down, so I lost my balance and was already falling to the floor.

I did as I was told. Sat cross-legged, and waited for her to speak once she had checked my work.

I can't remember now what she was trying to say, it was such an awful high-pitched noise. But I do clearly remember her throwing my book back at me.

Feeling so small, I sat with my head down. Ashamed and on the verge of tears, as the rest of the class laughed at me.

There I was, broken once again.

And now, I felt unsafe at school, as well as at home.

Staring at my workbook, pages open on the floor, and still with no explanation, I could definitely feel the tears coming. And the depth of the humiliation grew worse as I was ripped apart (verbally) in front of the whole class.

It wasn't the only time that this would happen. Shouting at me didn't make what I was being asked to do any clearer. It didn't help me in any way at all. Eventually I got used to it though.

My mum telling me afterwards that I must have deserved it made me think maybe it *was* my fault, and that I **did** deserve it.

But deep down I knew it wasn't right.

Everyone would look up and start laughing as I was told that I was stupid, and lazy, and I really **had** to start trying more.

Tears once again began to stream down my face as I was pushed back down onto the mat to sit with my book. I was still shocked by what had just happened, and still wondering what on earth I was supposed to be doing.

Why was this lady so mean to me? What have I done wrong? Why am I being treated differently?

Have you ever found yourself in a similar situation? Where you felt you were the only one going through it? Not understanding why, or even considering that it might actually turn out for the best over time.

Much later I discovered that I was not, in fact, the only one.

I guess I always kept my head down and didn't take much notice, because I didn't like loud noise or confrontation.

And I didn't like the thought of other people being made to feel sad. I knew only too well how that felt.

It turns out that my closest friend from then, my only real friend, had also experienced the same bullying back then from the same teacher. We shared our experiences over a drink when we unexpectedly bumped into each other 20 years later.

Ironically, my friend is now a lawyer.

****

As if that experience wasn't enough, now at the age of seven, I was doing my usual 30-minute walk home from school on my own (mum was never there to pick me up from school unlike so many of the other mums that were). It was coming to the end of term, and we were allowed to go home earlier than normal.

It was a beautiful sunny day, and I could smell the cut grass from the freshly mown lawns of all the houses on either side of the road as I wandered along, dreaming of what people's lives must be like who lived in those houses.

I can still picture those lines, even now, so precisely cut. Stripes up and down the gardens, like the old green and white Pacer Mints.

I don't think I was daydreaming as I walked along (something else I was often accused of). But I distinctly remember smiling, maybe even skipping.

Although I didn't necessarily want to rush home, I was so pleased to be out of school early that day, nevertheless.

I can also remember thinking that if I moved just a little bit faster at this point, I could easily get past the other school I had to walk by every day before they were let out for the day too.

I was wrong.

It was a high school where I'd learned, at my expense, that a terrifying group of bullies went.

As I approached the corner, I could see them coming towards me. I suddenly felt really hot. My little heart was pounding. And I was scared.

They got closer to me, so I quickly decided to cross the road to avoid any trouble.

But the gang of girls crossed over too. I had no escape.

They immediately started pushing me around. Shouting nasty things. Some things I didn't understand. Others, I did. Although at my age, I probably shouldn't have.

They continued. And then started spitting on me, tugging at my hair, and pulling on my bag until I tripped, and eventually fell to the ground.

It took me back to that day with Miss H, practically forcing me down onto the mat.

Then, as had happened so many times before, and would happen numerous times again in the future, those horrible girls simply walked away.

I could hear them screeching and laughing, as if they'd just been telling each other jokes, or were giggling stupidly over one of the boys who fancied one or other of them. But it wasn't that at all. It wasn't funny.

They left me there on the floor. Once again, ashamed and feeling small.

I got used to hiding my cuts, grazes, and multi-coloured bruises. Totally oblivious then, to the fact that this was all in preparation for my later life.

****

Mum used to tell me all the time that I would make nothing of myself. Even when I did well at sport, or managed to get good marks for a test (which wasn't very often), she would never celebrate it.

She'd say something about it being a one-off. Or they must have returned the wrong paper to me.

And so, not only did I keep quiet if I needed help, I soon got used to keeping it to myself if I had any good news too.

When we hear derogatory comments like that, time and time again, they become our truth. We start to believe, without question, that we are never going to be good enough.

As I lay in bed at night listening to the cars and the street noise, I would imagine myself all grown up. But homeless. You might think that's a strange concept to be 'happy' to visualise. And maybe so.

But feeling so unsafe at school, uncared for at home, and with a mother constantly telling me I would amount to nothing, homelessness didn't feel too bad as an alternative.

Please remember this was my 'child brain' thinking these thoughts. I appreciate now that homelessness isn't as I'd imagined it to be, and certainly not something I would wish on anybody. Even more so as I now volunteer at homeless shelters. And although I will never fully relate with what they are going through, I take the time to listen and help them to see they are not completely alone.

Many nights, I would lay there picturing the scene as I walked through the cold, wet streets, with just my blanket around me, and carrying a small plastic bag with a few old clothes. And yet, that still felt safer to me than the reality of my life at home.

I used to watch an Australian soap series filmed at the most beautiful beach. Some of you will know the one I mean. And I wished I had the life those kids were living there in front of me on the TV.

But one night, something completely random crossed my mind, and kind of stopped me in my thoughts for a minute.

'How will I still be able to watch my favourite TV show, and hold on to my dreams of escape, if I have no home to watch it in?'

My little head had become so mixed up and muddled, with everything going on around me.

Suddenly, I pictured myself looking through other people's windows, watching little girls with their mummies as they sat cosy together, giggling and cuddling.

I could see a vision of my dream life, and just a glimpse of *my* show on *their* television, through their window.

Crazy I know. Ironically, these days I don't even watch TV!

"The past cannot be changed and no one can determine your future. YOUR future is in YOUR power"
- Corinna Stringer

Chapter 2

The Wind Beneath My Wings

Despite the lack of love and comfort I was receiving at home, from the one person I should have been able to rely on it coming from, luckily for me growing up, I did however have the most fantastic influencers. And I would, adoringly, spend every weekend and holiday with them.

My grandparents.

They supported me in whatever I did and they each taught me so much.

My grandad would take me to the auction, markets and car boot sales, where we became an unstoppable force to be reckoned with! Everybody knew us, we came as a pair, selling all sorts of old bits and bobs.

I can still smell those markets now, and the cigar that my grandad used to burn down to his lip! See what I mean about the brain storing things, whether they are words or feelings associated with experiences?

The strong stench of copper pennies and two pence coins.

It made me chuckle watching the customers empty their pockets or coin bags into their rough, wrinkled, yellowish orange tobacco-stained fingers and blackened hands. They would spend ages counting up, adding each coin carefully to the pile. Only to realise they were still about 10 pence short of what grandad would sell it to them for!

Sometimes he would back down. Especially if there was a cheeky glint in the customer's eye, or if he felt sorry for them. Other times, he firmly stood his ground, knowing he would find a full-price buyer somewhere for it.

He would say to me, "Right, we bought this hammer for 50 pence, and we're selling it for a pound, so how much profit will we make?"

If I gave him the right answer, I was allowed to keep the profit. And as some of the customers thought I was cute, they would give me a few more pennies too.

I can remember him watching me on another occasion put up a sign when I wanted to sell some of my nan's clothes. They'd had a market stall since way before I was born, so there were always plenty of bags of clothes to sell.

Anyway, I'd hung the clothes up on a rail, and he let me write this sign all nice and neat, thinking I'd done such a great job – *50p each or 2 for £1* – it raised a wry smile or two. Some of the punters fell for it and thought they'd got a great bargain! Some gave me the pound anyway, just for my cheekiness and excitement for being there!

Precious memories are often made from what can seem like the most mundane experiences to some. But I absolutely loved spending this time with my grandad.

He taught me the value of money, but also the most important thing for me all those years ago… how to always make the best out of what we have.

That makes me laugh now, too. Especially as it's not so many months ago that I took myself off to a market to sell some bits. Sitting behind the table, with neat piles of "stuff" laid out there for all to see. It took me back to our times all those years ago.

Mind you, the sun was shining much warmer than it used to shine back then, and we had a huge golfing umbrella, so we could sit in the shade. It was luxury in comparison!

But the rest of the experience felt the same. Oh, other than using a card machine, at which grandad would be turning in his grave!

My nan, well, she ran the house. She was a strong, resolute, and powerful woman. Small, but effective, you could say!

She was born just before the war, and had been evacuated to Yorkshire. They always said that the children who were placed with other families during the war grew up quicker, because they had to learn a whole new way of life. Nan grew up very quickly. Her sister was born not long after the war, around the same time as curfews were lifted, life was returning to a new normality, and her parents got their freedom back! Needless to say, nan was able to 'keep house' perfectly before she reached her teens.

I loved listening to the tales of her days living on a farm up in Yorkshire. It must have been special to her, because even in her 80's if she was talking about it, her face lit up, a little twinkle appeared in her eye, and her voice used to change to a sort of Cockney London accent mixed with a Yorkshire twang.

It was my nan, I guess, who nurtured my determination and drive. Possibly also the kind, caring, and sarcastic nature I've been told I display! How ever you see me though, I'm so proud to say I take after her.

Grandad was a very active man who enjoyed gardening and generally being outdoors. He never believed in working set hours. He would be up at the crack of dawn to get all the best bargains on the markets, and then get home whenever he had done all he possibly could to make sure he and nan had the best life possible. In other words, he worked flippin' hard for his money and for his family.

In addition to taking me to car boot sales and weekend markets, he also loved going to local auctions where he was a well-known character – both buying and selling all sorts. My nan would always say to him "What on earth did you buy *that* for?" as he piled more and more boxes into the garage. They loved each other to bits, but boy did they bicker!

I thought it was hilarious, and would stand behind her giggling and pulling faces at grandad, knowing that whatever he'd bought that day, he'd sell the next week at a different market for more than double the price he had paid for it. He had a knack with sales. And his customers loved him.

After a long day, having been out in all weather, I remember coming home to my grandparents' house. The warmth would hit me as I opened the front door, and we'd all smile to see each other. Just content to be safe and back in each other's company.

I know on some occasions, it was the heat from the kitchen as we walked in and saw the freshly-prepared roast dinner my nan would have spent hours cooking for us. A sense of loving warmth, safety, and security radiated from every room in that house.

Perhaps it was my desperation to feel wrapped up in those emotions that heightened their love for me even more. I never felt so important, so much a part of someone's life, as I did when I was with my nan and grandad.

Now I really appreciate what people mean when they say being in someone's company feels like time is standing still. That's how it was for me whenever I was with them.

It's precious memories like this that take us back. The smell of roast dinners cooking, cakes baking, or freshly hung washing blowing in the breeze. Remember what I said earlier about a scene or a fragrance taking us right back to those moments, and remind us of happy times.

I sometimes wear items that belonged to my nan even now. She worked in fashion and there was something special for me about her style.

When I was sorting their wardrobes and drawers not so long ago, I came across loads of beautiful clothes still with the labels on (it wasn't that she was frivolous with her money at all, I hasten to add!) Many of them are making a comeback now. Whenever I wear something that belonged to her, I get the most amazing compliments. And, despite some very strange looks and sideways glances I get, I'm not at all ashamed to tell people it was my nan's.

Of course, as I said, I loved being around my nan and grandad. I adored doing anything with them. And I know they felt the same about me.

But the true depth of their love for me, and how much they had inspired my life, only became clear to me many years later.

A couple of my nan's favourite phrases were, "If you can't laugh about it, you'll cry," and "God pays debts without money."

Nan had such a way with words. And I laugh now because they seemed to be so personal to her, so old fashioned, yet many of them still ring true today.

In a similar way, we don't always appreciate the value of those truly special relationships at the time. It becomes easy to take them for granted.

Another thing we should learn from.

Chapter 3

Learning to Forgive to Let Go

I was like the third cog in my grandparent's wheel of life. Is that how you describe it? Anyway, I was a major part of their being.

We were so close, in fact, that my nan said she was worried I was going to be born on grandad's birthday, which would make me more of a birthday present to him, than a gift of a grandchild to them both.

Grandad's birthday was the 17th July, I appeared on the 15th. Both typical Cancerians, compassionate, nurturing, and loved our homes. Grandad had been getting a bit cocky about sharing our birthday as the date got closer, but my nan got her way!

One of the best celebrations we ever had was my 21st and his 70th. He tried to tell me I was a year older than him, with his age ending in a zero and mine ending in a one!

Perhaps they did see me as an adult then?

I know they saw a lot more in me than either mum or I saw. And it made me want to be a better person. It drove me to be successful, and to aim for my destiny. Even if it took me a few years, and I detoured off the runway a couple of times, before I found my path!

Despite the bond with my grandparents, you're probably picking up on the fact that the relationship with my mother, on the other hand, was not exactly great.

I couldn't understand why, or how, she could be so different from my nan.

In fact, nan once admitted she wondered what on earth she'd done that was so bad, for her daughter to turn out the way she did.

I now know and appreciate that people are not their behaviour. Just because they may behave or react in a certain way, it doesn't define them. We can't always explain why some people do the things they do.

Maybe mum had always been one of those people who thought she had to fight for attention? Did she think she always had to fight against that feeling of never being good enough? And so she had to overcompensate in many other ways?

Whatever she did, it must have come across in a way other people couldn't or didn't want to understand. Not many people ever understood her when I was growing up.

I can only assume she also told herself that it was a good enough reason to behave the way she did to me. I don't say this with any bitterness, even though I used to feel that way. I just doubt I will ever get her version of events. And all I ever saw was the most unpleasant, distant, side of her character.

It turns out she didn't have many genuine friends either. And was often the odd one out in the groups she tried to fit into. Even the ones she house-shared with didn't particularly want her around.

In preparing for this publication, and my other eBooks, presentations, and learning resources, I have also done much reflecting. I have spent hours of personal development time processing moments, memories, and experiences from childhood and onwards throughout my life.

But in all of this, one thing I *can't* remember, is any time when I truly felt loved by mum. Or that I could ever hold her attention for any significant length of time.

I have previously mentioned that she would let me play in the same room as her for a little while. And it was fine when I was her waitress, serving the party drinks and snacks. But as soon as something more interesting (usually a man) appeared, then I was pushed out of the way and told to be quiet.

I played hockey during high school, and I was a bit feisty on the pitch. One day I was hit on the edge of my eye as one of the other girls swung her stick going in for a tackle.

It wasn't pleasant at all.

Apparently, there was a trail of blood all the way from the pitch to the changing rooms. Apologies if you're squeamish, or triggered by this, but I need you to get the full picture of how nasty it was.

Anyway, I sat with a bag of frozen peas from the canteen on my eye to try and ease the swelling and reduce some of the pain.

It was so bad that I was slipping in and out of consciousness.

School called mum several times (I think they said it was about five in total), yet it still took her almost three hours to finally pick me up. I wasn't surprised. In fact, I was expecting to get taken to hospital in a taxi, and for her to show up when everything was sorted out.

Apparently, it was made very clear in the last attempt to call her that the situation would 'escalate' if she didn't come to collect me immediately.

I don't know what the excuse was this time for her noticeable absence but she eventually turned up (thanks to her 'then' partner driving her to pick me up) and we finally got to the hospital.

(Potential trigger here, so continue to the next paragraph if hospital scenes are not your thing).

By this time, the inevitable concussion had set in.

I was starting to feel really queasy, so I asked for help to get to the toilet. Help didn't arrive quickly enough.

As soon as I moved, I was sick. And I mean projectile. Only it wasn't just a normal kind of sick that would be expected with a concussion. I was throwing up black blood. And I was scared.

Cue mum going into full-blown drama queen mode, "Oh my darling daughter. Somebody, help her!" Arms flailing everywhere. So over the top.

In her (weak) attempts to show the nursing staff, and said partner, some sort of affection towards me, she demanded a wheelchair, and that I was to be seen immediately.

I couldn't care less about the wheelchair. I just wanted the pain to go away and to stop feeling sick. And for her to shut up!

Anyway, after a while, it was too much for mum to take. As soon as she mentioned that Eastenders would be on soon, we knew she'd be gone. Nothing could keep her away from her soaps!

So, I was left at the hospital with her partner. Which, ironically, turned out better than if mum had stayed with me – at least we spoke and had a sensible conversation! And bless him, he tried to comfort me, far more genuinely than mum had ever done, or ever would.

I was laid there on a drip, in the hospital bed, as he looked at me, clearly shocked.

"I can't believe your mum just did that," he said. And I could feel how sorry he was, both because of the state I was in, and for the fact that he'd now also seen her at her least caring.

As a family, we all found out so much about my mum during this time. I'd already seen and experienced so many examples of her selfish, and what I now believe to be, narcissistic behaviour.

But it was my nan I felt sorry for. She had always been shielded somehow from mum's ways. She never saw the complete disconnect between my mum and me. No sympathy. Never any affection towards me. Or perhaps she did, but she didn't want to accept it was real. *How could her daughter be so cold?*

I hadn't particularly warmed to this guy at first, nor any of mum's male friends really. In my eyes, they were another distraction. Each one, just another reason to be somewhere else. Somewhere away from where she should be, and could have been – with me. But, like a puppy will always return to its master even if it is mistreated, I still wanted my mum to be there, and was glad when she came back. And like that puppy, I would keep bounding back to her after she'd pushed me away again.

Over time, though, this guy and I became quite good friends.

We even stayed in contact for a while after they split up. He had a printer and helped me with my CVs when I started applying for jobs. And it seemed as though he was genuinely pleased to have someone to talk to. Someone he could share his frustrations with about his relationship with my mum.

Sadly, he was honest enough to admit he knew she'd only been with him for his money. Or at least the money she *thought* he would inherit imminently, as his father was seriously ill.

For all she did to me (or didn't, as the case may be) it was still hard to hear someone else saying things like that about my mum.

As I said, I always wanted to trust and believe in her, and see the best in her, as with everyone. But that's not always the best thing to do. Particularly when you start to see repeat patterns of negative behaviour, ending in the same negative outcome every time.

In my case, I would get let down over and over.

I want to highlight again here that people are not defined by their behaviour. And I do not hold anything against my mum now.

I've gone through hours and hours of inner work, and studied psychology and how our minds operate. And with the help of Neuro-Linguistic Programming, I realise now that what mum was doing was for the best. She thought she was protecting me. That was *her* truth.

She was protecting herself from rejection first and foremost, by pushing anyone away who came close. She would create the distance before they could, based on her assumption from the past that she would be left on the side lines.

And then, she started conditioning me to be the same. I put up with her narcissistic behaviour for so long. But it became too much for me eventually, and I no longer have a relationship with her.

Wherever she had felt pushed out, she learned from it. She wanted me to be strong and independent enough to be able to handle the same situation if it ever happened to me.

The thing was, as a child, all I saw was her keeping me away from friends. In a way, she was keeping me to herself. Keeping me small. Not letting me shine my light, even at the few things I was good at. And then, when I was of no use to her, she'd push me to one side.

Ironically, I can finally now see that it did make me stronger, as it so often does.

It felt more often as though I was the parent in the relationship with mum. I had to grow up quickly, just like my nan.

Before I reached my teens, I was very much independent, and often left alone in the house whilst mum was going through one of her many self-destructive periods.

I'd watched nan so often in the kitchen, that I was capable of cooking for myself. And I'd always plate a meal up for mum, just in case she came back.

Then, I would spend hours keeping busy by hoovering, and wiping the windows. I'd clean the windowsill once, twice, maybe even three times, and move ornaments around to see where they looked best.

Little did I know at the time that this habitual cleaning was my coping mechanism when I was anxious. Nor that it would eventually help ease the OCD that had formed within this vicious cycle.

Remember, we do things based on past experiences. But also consider that your experiences are not the same as anyone else's.

What has happened to you might not make sense.

You replay it over and over in your mind, wondering if you'd done something different, would the outcome have been different?

Look at it this way though. All that does is take up your time and energy. Both of which you could be using on something more positive and more productive.

In my case, mum did things that upset me. And although it doesn't make it right, the best thing I ever did, once I'd moved on from my inner child brain, was to learn how to **forgive**.

There are a few things you probably need to know about forgiveness before you start shouting at the page, and questioning how you can ever be expected to forgive someone who has brought such hurt and heartache to you in your life.

Forgiveness doesn't mean you can change the past.

Nor does it mean you (ever) have to welcome those people who hurt you back into your life with open arms. You don't even have to speak to them again if you don't want to.

And finally, forgiving doesn't mean you will suddenly start to look back on bad situations with fondness or even happiness.

What it does mean, is that you can process the experience, reframe it and see it from a different perspective.

Forgiveness means you release the bad energy and bad vibration that's been stored in your body and your mind for too long.

The way I work with my clients now on forgiveness and release allows us to free up space and create a renewed energy to focus on greater things. In essence, the event or experience is still there - it doesn't magically vanish! What we do, though, is remove the negative energy and emotional attachment that has been tied to that event or experience, using the phenomenal modality of Emotional Change Therapy.

It means you can then move forward to a reshaped future, taking account of your learnings, and with the ability to allow positive energy to flow.

My own experiences have taught me so many things which I have now been able to reframe in the same way, and I'll come back to within the 'learnings' section later in the book.

What about you?

Have you been through something similar? Something that's causing you to hold on to bitterness, resentment, or other negative emotions?

How we do anything is how we do everything, right?

So, if you are handling one area of your life in a particular way i.e. with negative energy in this case, does that mean you are also doing the same in your business too?

Is what you have experienced causing you to behave in a certain way? And do you wish you could change it somehow?

Can you reframe what has happened in your past, to create a new perspective for your future?

If there could be a resolution to family, relationship, or even business issues, please take note of my learnings, and learn from them yourself.

Being open to deep-rooted inner work and acknowledgment of who you are and what you have been through, could reveal (and release) so much for you.

You might also be surprised to learn how it could change your entire life. Not just from a personal relationship perspective. But also give a boost to your business.

I'll say it again – how we do anything is how we do everything.

Now, I can tell you that it takes a strong person to step back and allow their perspective to change. But it can create so much positivity out of an historic negative, possibly even toxic, situation.

It creates a space to look forward and focus on your goals without that same burden you've been holding onto.

You will have the chance to think about your goals in a later chapter. So prepare for that!

For me, the reality of finally seeing one of my goals come to fruition in writing this chapter has been quite cathartic.

Getting the thoughts out of my head and onto paper with the acknowledgement that I have moved on from the childhood 'trauma' and a lifestyle that, sadly, I'm sure some of you can resonate with, has been huge.

It has played a leading role in the act of learning to love myself once again. Through which I have also been able to commit to forgiving others, and myself, in the process.

Love is just one example of a deeply profound emotion. Strong enough that it can hide us from the truth, distort reality, and give us an entirely false perspective.

How about you? Are you feeling a connection with your life experiences?

Have your cards dealt you a hand that still impacts your progress?

Does holding onto negativity from your past bring your world crashing down at times?

Perhaps it was love for my mum that prevented my nan from seeing how I was raised. It might have even been a deep (hidden) love for me that made my mum treat me the way she did.

But I knew other people weren't the same. I saw other children living completely different lives. My mum wasn't happy and popular like their mums. My mum was never there at the school gate to pick me up, or there cheering me on at sports day.

And unknowingly, this treatment and my reaction to it as I grew up, then attracted many more similar relationships in which I was to be tested, taken advantage of, but by default brought through the other side with valuable messages to share.

"Someone may have handed you the poison many years ago, but why do you continue to drink it?"

Chapter 4

Flying High 'til I Hit the Ground

My grandad had been suffering from cancer for many years.

Doctors had managed to control it for a while. But, in 2010, at the same time as I was engaged to the love of my life, and all seemed to be going amazingly for me, grandad's cancer came back. Aggressively.

I remember the day so clearly. A day that was filled with the most all-consuming and crushing sadness. Yet, somehow, also an overwhelming sense of relief.

My fiancé and I were sitting at the dining room table when I got the call. The call that I had been dreading for weeks.

"Hello?"

My heart felt like it was beating right out of my chest. I can still remember my hands shaking as I held my phone. And then came the words that I knew were inevitable, but I would have given anything at that moment, to not hear them.

"It's mum. You need to come to the hospital."

In reality, she didn't need to say anything at all. Just the fact she had taken the time and made the effort to call me told me everything. We were hardly speaking by then, so there would be no other conceivable reason for her to ring me.

We done shifts, spending day and night by grandad's bedside throughout the previous few weeks.

Sometimes he would chat away, telling stories of his younger days. And I would sit with my arms on the edge of the bed, smiling with every single word he said. For once, the time didn't stand still in his company like it used to. Quite the opposite. The hours, days, and nights passed so quickly. I never wanted him to stop talking.

Yet, the next day, he wouldn't know who we were, or that we were even there in the room with him.

The evening of that call, we were all chatting away around his bed. Laughing to lighten the reality of what we knew was to come. Filling the void of what could have been the most uncomfortable hours.

His heavy breathing was accompanied by the beep of the machines in the background, and the noise from the intermittent buzzers that other patients were still capable of using to call for attention.

Grandad loved a good cuppa. Another trait I seem to have picked up by the bucketload! But, by now, he could only take liquids from a small sponge stick that we dripped onto his lips.

I'd made his favourite milky tea. Two sugars to nicely sweeten the taste, exactly as he liked it.

I leaned over, and as I put it to his mouth, he grabbed my hand and sucked the sponge so hard that his cheeks and lips were all scrunched up. I giggled. He looked almost childlike in that split second. But it was lovely to see the sheer delight in his eyes.

I felt blessed to have been able to experience that moment of connection, and to know that precious memory would never fade.

As I took the sponge away, he smiled. It was that gentle kind of content, 'knowing' smile. And I knew right then, too, that this would be his last cup of tea.

A few hours later, I went outside for some 'fresh air.' Well, that's what I had to call it, considering none of the family knew I smoked. Or at least they never admitted to me that they knew.

As I sat on the bench outside the hospital, I suddenly shivered, yet felt this warm, overwhelming feeling of calm.

I immediately looked up at my fiancé who had come outside with me, and explained to him how this wave of peace had just come over me. It literally filled and surrounded my body from head to toe. I felt a massive release.

You know when you've been so intently concentrating on something that you haven't even breathed? You suddenly stop and breathe in as deeply to your belly as you can, and then slowly and completely let it go?

This moment felt just like that.

As we walked back into the room, my nan was standing in the doorway.

She was also clearly at peace, and her face seemed somehow less wrinkled than I remember it being only moments before.

With a gentle cough to clear her throat, she said those two words that will forever stay etched in my memory, "He's gone."

There were no dramatic scenes, or an almost anticipated wailing from my mum.

Despite wanting to grab hold of him and hug him tightly to ease some of the pain, we all simply let him be.

We started to pack up grandad's things. And we said our goodbyes, so tenderly.

Then, at that last moment, just as it felt we were all still there in the room together, the strangest thing happened.

There was a radio on the nightstand, which had been silent the entire time grandad was in that hospital. For some reason, it just hadn't ever worked. But, from out of nowhere, and right on cue, it suddenly came on at the same time as the ceiling lights started to flicker.

Although I saw this as his final goodbye, his cheeky sense of humour playing tricks with us all just when we needed it, it was also his way of telling me to watch out for signs in the future that he will still be with me.

And then, just as quickly once again, everything was still, quiet, and back to normal.

As normal as it could ever be without the one man in my life who had given so much, without ever asking for anything from me in return.

Nan's words ran through my head once more, as I thought, "*Yes, he's gone.*"

This was the start of me hitting the ground with what turned out to be a very big bang.

Chapter 5

Shattered Wings

By now I had my own home, a great career, and a loving fiancé.

Life was good. Yes, we had some issues at home, but most couples do, don't they? We were due to get married the following year, and we would get through these niggles. We'd be fine.

There's a decades-old phrase, another of nan's favourites, "it never rains, but it pours."

Well, it wasn't just about to rain on me. It would pour. Torrential, in fact! And I was yet to discover darker times that would test my good nature and emotional strength to their limits.

I wasn't really sure how to respond to my grandad's passing. I'd never felt grief like it before.

What was I supposed to do? What was I supposed to say? How was I supposed to be?

I'd sit and stare for hours at the TV, or into thin air, without a single thought going through my mind.

Or maybe they did, but they must have been those thoughts that weren't worth processing or storing away somewhere, so they just drifted on through without me knowing.

I was strong on the outside to people who knew my nan and grandad, and would ask, "How's your family doing?"

Was it selfish of me, that on the inside, I was desperate to scream out *"and ME? What about ME?"*

It had come to a head the day after we lost grandad.

I'd called my nan to see how she was. It seemed they'd made plans of their own. My aunt was coming over, and they'd decided to go out for the day shopping and probably grab some lunch, to take their minds off everything.

I can only assume that they thought I would be ok too, with my fiancé by my side to look after me.

I probably wouldn't have gone with them anyway, especially as mum would have been there attention-grabbing. But that feeling of being pushed to the side … again … was more than I could take this time.

What I hadn't mentioned to them, nor to you yet, was that when I'd received that call to go to the hospital, my fiancé and I were in the middle of an argument.

It had been a huge row. I'd even reached the point of wrenching my engagement ring off my finger.

I'd gradually started to appreciate the extent of the damage that my childhood had caused, when we began to row over anything and everything to do with his ex-partner. I would pick fault with everything. I'd get snappy. My mood would change literally in a split second the instant his ex was even mentioned, let alone made contact with him. It just felt like she was still controlling the relationship, and he would let her.

He had a little girl from that relationship, who I absolutely adored.

The thing was, he would always let me down at the last minute because of something she'd done, or arrangements his ex-partner had made and forgotten to tell us, or deliberately left it until too late for us to do anything to help. He would get upset and go out without me to let off steam.

Now I look back, I wonder if this was my mind generalising?

Did he always let me down? Or did he do it a couple of times, and I just remembered those occasions, rather than all the lovely things he did for me the rest of the time? Had I made everything so much worse, just because of what I was expecting to happen?

That's how the mind distorts the facts, too. Not easy, is it?

Going back to the argument and the day after grandad died. It was there again, clear as day, my attachment issue. Leaving me feeling like that little Corinna, being pushed to the side even now by the love of my life!

I can't remember the details or how the argument had started, but it blew out of all proportion and I blurted out something like, "It's her or me!"

He was, quite rightly, on the defensive. His interpretation was completely different from my intention, and he immediately assumed I was trying to get him to choose between me and his daughter.

I would never have done that and that wasn't what I meant at all.

Anyway, I yanked my ring off, telling him I couldn't be engaged to him right now. I meant I just couldn't deal with this right now, knowing how close we were to losing my grandad.

And with that, the call came through.

Nothing was going to get in the way of me and my grandad, not even an argument like this. I knew what I wanted to say, and thought we would be able to clear the air later.

Obviously, he came to the hospital with me, as I couldn't have driven anyway. And as it happened, I was in no state to carry on the conversation when we got home that night either.

So, as I was on the phone with nan, hearing about their shopping trip, my fiancé was upstairs, getting ready for work.

He never used to work on a Saturday. But this particular day, of all days, he did. Well, he said that was where he was going, and I had no reason to doubt him. He probably needed some space anyway, it had been a pretty heavy couple of days.

As I sat and waited for him to come downstairs, the silence in my head was palpable. I wanted to take it and throw it into the river along with all the hurt that I was feeling in my heart.

Not only was I dealing with the massive loss of my grandad. The man who had raised me like his own daughter, and taught me so much about life, expectations, and reality.

But something else wasn't quite right in me.

I didn't know what it was or how to describe it. Nor did I know at the time that I was heading for something else that would completely shatter my wings.

This strange feeling of uneasiness felt like it was squashing me. Crushing me.

He popped his head in to say goodbye, seeming calm and very matter-of-fact. Just like normal.

But as he stepped out of the front door, he turned around to where I was standing, like I usually did to kiss him goodbye.

He came straight out with it. Stood there and told me he was leaving me.

Is this really happening? I mean, right now? Not that there's ever a "best" time to be told something quite as soul-destroying. But why now?

I was devastated. I went numb. Even more numb than I already was from the previous day's experience.

And suddenly, there I was. I felt like I had no one.

I didn't tell anybody, as my family had a lot to deal with already. And I hadn't yet recovered from my fear of asking for help or support of any kind. So, I kept it to myself.

Maybe, deep down, I hoped he would come back and tell me it was all ok.

I was still numb when he came round a few days later to collect some of his stuff. At which point he also chose to tell me he didn't love me anymore and there was no point trying to work things out now.

He agreed to come to the funeral with me. And I showed up with a brave face on.

Underneath the surface, though, I was doing what we so often do. I was carrying the weight of an excruciatingly painful and heavy heart but refused to let it show in front of anyone.

I'm not sure whether having him there made things easier or harder. There was no way I was going to lean on my mum for emotional strength. I wasn't going to add extra emotion onto my nan's shoulders either. But I knew I needed someone. I couldn't face it on my own.

We were sitting at the garden side of the building. I can remember looking through the full-length windows of the newly-constructed church, staring aimlessly, thinking how beautiful that we should be on this side, when grandad loved his garden so much. He was still pottering around, tending to his beloved plants and shrubs well past his retirement.

I forced myself to look away from the service and the congregation in case I caught anyone's eye. And I wanted to somehow distance myself from everything going on inside.

"Don't start crying, Corinna. You'll show yourself up. You'll make a fool of yourself. And you'll never be able to stop."

Even in those moments, in the deepest, darkest sadness I'd ever felt, those inner voices were still telling me the worst about myself. They might have had a point this time though.

Stories of my grandad's life were being told. They didn't have that same joy though that I used to feel when grandad told me his tales himself. And when I heard his favourite songs being played, they didn't sound the same either.

But then came my poem.

I knew the order of service, so knew it was coming next. Still, when the Vicar started to read W.H. Auden's "Stop All the Clocks," I melted in my seat.

It's a well-known poem that I had heard in school many years before. You may recognise it, too, from a certain even more well-known movie from the 1990's.

I instantly thought of it for my grandad and felt it was very personal. But I'd changed it slightly to relate it to how I remembered him now:

Stop all the clocks, cut off the telephone,
Prevent the dog from barking with a juicy bone,
Silence the Harp and with muffled drum
Bring out the coffin, let the mourners come.
Let aeroplanes circle moaning overhead

Scribbling in the sky, the message that he left …

Be happy, not sad, for now, I'm at rest,

Keep me close in your hearts and plant that cherry tree where I said,

REMEMBER I'm still with you every step of the way,

Although you can't see me, I'll still be there on all those special days.

He was my North, my South, my East, and West,

My working week and my Sunday rest,

My noon, my midnight, my talk, my song

He had the true strength of a STRINGER,

He taught me right from wrong.

The stars are up there, bright in the sky,

So, say "ta-ta" for now, dry your eyes, don't cry.

He'll light up a cigar and take the dog for a walk,

So now fold up this poem and seal it with the letters S.W.A.L.K (sealed with a loving kiss) xxx

****

And with that, grandad was gone.

Chapter 6

The Black Box

For many months after the funeral, I became more and more withdrawn from the outside world. It felt like I was in a huge bubble, looking out, just watching everyone else.

By the time grandad had become really ill, I had already accepted that I'd probably been suffering from depression since childhood. Not to mention the OCD that had also become my coping mechanism for so many moments and experiences. I also knew by then that I needed help. I didn't go down that route straight away though. I had already learned to overcome much of my childhood trauma, and learned from it. So, like I said, I wasn't ready to ask for support from anyone.

Over a period of about the next six months, my health started to suffer badly. I had fallen into a deep downward spiral, couldn't be bothered to eat properly or take care of myself. As a result, I kept having to take days off sick.

I'd often suffered with throat infections and whenever I got excessively tired, run down, or emotionally impacted by something significant, I could guarantee

Tonsillitis would strike. Needless to say, this was happening a lot.

I didn't want to be at work. In fact, I didn't really want to be anywhere.

And it became noticeable to those at work, at least, that I had lost a disturbing amount of weight.

I kind of knew I was getting skinny at the time. But it was only when I saw some photos of me at a family celebration a few years later, that I realised how bad I looked. It probably didn't help that I'd decided to dye my hair black. And even though there was a smile on my face, I can still see the pain that was behind my eyes.

Always one to find a positive though, it was great to find out I could finally squeeze back into my skinny jeans! (Not that the excitement about that lasted too long. It was only about another year before I could barely breathe in the damn things again!)

Speaking of always finding a positive (or laughing so I didn't cry, as nan encouraged me to do) I even laughed the day my trousers almost fell down at work. Ironically, it was as I stood up because my manager had called me into the office for a chat. One of "those" chats – you know the ones I mean?

Head Office was 'concerned' about my sales figures and the fact I didn't seem to have the same enthusiasm for the job. Where had this young woman gone who was once one of the top sales staff, and always seen as so welcoming and helpful to the customers? Oh, and I should be careful, I was looking ill. Oh, and yes, looking at the numbers my sick days were increasing. Oh, and another thing (talk about kicking a girl when she's down) I was losing far too much weight. That was it, in a nutshell. They were basically telling me I was a bloody big mess!

They were right.

Every day, sparking up another cigarette and downing another bottle of wine, my drinking got worse as well. I had never been a big drinker, but it's easy to get into a habit. I didn't want to head down that route but I so desperately wanted the pain and sadness to go away.

I honestly felt I had nothing left. And what little I did have, was caught up in the midst of my self-destruction plan.

Have you ever reached that point in your life when it seems to move so quickly, that you feel completely out of control? Everything is swirling around you. Happening *to* you, seemingly without a choice.

Sometimes we need to hit absolute rock bottom before coming back up.

Looking back now, it was so obvious. But back then I didn't have a clue what was going on. I was in that bubble of nothingness. Numbness.

Please know, I am not talking about these times in a pity party way at all. When you are stuck in the middle of something that feels so empty, though, this is exactly how it feels.

I want you to realise that there is a way out. "This, too, shall pass." Something I have learned to remind myself whenever I have a down day.

Anyway, I was a mess at work. No better at home. Then one day, I just couldn't take any more.

If you had seen me then, sitting on my kitchen floor, pills in one hand and bottle in the other, it was like I had become someone else. This 'other' person had physically taken over my body, and I had absolutely no control.

As each pill was dropped into my mouth, I felt an increasingly overwhelming sense of calm.

The last time I had felt that same calm flood through my body, was the day my grandad left us. Knowing there was no more pain and suffering.

Is that how it feels to slowly let yourself drift away?

But in a split second of clarity, I realised what I was doing.

And with that, as if grandad was there to stop me, just in case I didn't stop myself, the front door flew open.

You'll start to see that I am one of those firm believers that everything happens for a reason. And as I mentioned earlier, those signs we experience are there for a reason too.

Every person we meet, and every situation that tests us, all happen for a reason that is way beyond our comprehension.

We certainly don't know it at the time, but the more we learn to trust those signals, the ones that tell us we are on the right path or heading in the right direction, and to trust our intuition, the clearer life becomes.

****

It was Christmas day, 2010. I'd been with my family, and it was less than two months since my grandad had passed.

From the moment I woke up, I knew it was going to be a strange day. The firsts of everything after a bereavement or loss of any kind are always the worst, aren't they?

I had kept it to myself leading up to Christmas that my fiancé had left me. And, thankfully, it wasn't inconceivable that he wouldn't be joining us for our day, as my family knew he would want to be with his little girl.

We really missed grandad's knack of keeping the banter going at the dinner table though, and as the general chit-chat quietened and the tacky Christmas cracker jokes had all been told, so the atmosphere got a bit awkward.

Nan mentioned something about not having seen him for a while, so I finally admitted that my fiancé had left, and I was back on my own, I don't think it came as too much of a surprise to her. She just gave a little sympathetic nod of acknowledgement when I made it clear I wanted that to be the end of the subject.

Mum, in her typical 'couldn't care less about anyone else' approach, kept trying to goad me, pretending she was genuinely concerned. She was not breaking me. Not today. And I was having none of it.

And I was right. Because I later found out that she'd said she wasn't surprised he left me, and that I'd probably cheated on him. In her true to form harsh words, he deserved better than me.

Some things never change. But I wonder if this was her generalising due to her own experiences?

As soon as we'd finished eating, I made my excuses and left. I needed to get out of there and be by myself. Even though I didn't actually want to be by myself. Does that make sense?

My ex-fiancé called me on the way home though, and we ended up having a heated discussion about collecting the rest of his stuff. I'd blamed him for how everything around me was falling apart.

We didn't argue as such. I didn't have the energy to fight. I kept prodding. Digging away. I desperately wanted him to tell me how he could have just walked away, without any sign of remorse. How could he have done that? We were supposed to be getting married! And the day after my grandad had died!

It was all too much.

As I sat in my car on the drive, tears streaming down my face, I could barely see. I needed air. I felt suffocated. I couldn't breathe. Struggling to find the handle to get out of the car, I started to panic. I got more and more upset, as my breathing became more and more erratic.

Just about managing to crawl to the front door, every step I took demanded more of my energy. The energy I didn't have. I had to lean on the car, on the wall, my knees were giving way beneath me. My hands were shaking. And I felt so incredibly empty.

He came round to the house soon after, and the conversation continued. He threw together what was left of his belongings, and stormed out.

I had never felt more abandoned.

One of those inner voices sparked up, *"Corinna, what's the point?"*

Knocking everything else out the way – the wine glasses, tea-stained mugs, teaspoons, and used, dried out teabags that had by now been there for days – I picked up the bottles from the kitchen worktop. As I did so, I let my exhausted body slide down the cupboard doors and slip to the kitchen floor. I had become weaker, in so many ways.

This was the final straw.

Moments later, though, in that same instant I caught myself at my weakest moment, there was a loud bang and the front door burst open.

Had he not shut it properly as he slammed out of the house earlier? Had he been knocking and I hadn't heard him as I slumped to the floor, drowning my sorrows?

Either way, he was back again, and it didn't matter how.

He found me sitting there, a crumpled heap on the ground.

I was dizzy. I felt hot. And I could barely see who it was. I just knew somebody was there with me. And for once in my life, it was just when I needed them the most.

Thankfully, he worked out what I had done with what could have been a lethal concoction of alcohol and pills. I couldn't tell him how much drink I had consumed or how many tablets I'd taken, and before I knew it his fingers were down my throat. Forcing me to bring it all back up again.

He didn't stop until he thought my stomach was clear. I felt disgusted. Weak. Frail. Embarrassed.

Although he stayed that night, I already knew he wasn't staying any longer than that.

He would leave, and he would never come back again.

Why would he want to? How could this sad, repulsive body be of any interest to anyone? Let alone be physically attractive to anyone.

I literally was a shadow of the outwardly confident and successful Corinna he had first met. But my inner problems had become too much for him to handle.

And if *I* couldn't work my way through my own life, why should anyone else want to help me?

I felt so low, and saw myself as a huge burden on him and anyone else around me.

Here I was, utterly ashamed that I was failing to cope. Bitterly disappointed that I hadn't had the chance to go through with what I had started.

I'd known something was wrong, but had no idea of the severity of the depression that had led me to the attempted suicide.

There, I said the words.

****

Two months later, I started therapy. It actually made me feel worse.

One-to-one counselling. Group therapy sessions. You name it, I had it.

The medication I had been prescribed was making me so tired. Each day I felt as though I was living in a haze of what should have been my life. I should have been in my prime. In my twenties, my whole life ahead of me.

Yet, like me, my life was now barely recognisable.

Acceptance, and allowing yourself to grieve for any loss, is a massive part of recovery.

When we break a bone, we're not expected to "just walk it off." So why do we allow ourselves to feel bad for taking the time to repair our minds? In fact, we seem to think it can be done with a few chats, or half a dozen sessions with a therapist.

When we start to feel worse, which is quite often what happens before any big improvement, we beat ourselves up about it even more. Not going back to this group, or to speak to that therapist. They're not helping me.

What we should do is rest and let the muscles and bones repair. It takes time and is a natural process that cannot, and should never, be rushed.

The same can be said for our minds too.

I remember one therapy session in particular. I was asked about my relationship with my mum. I was fine talking about it—possibly something to do with the numbness I was experiencing from the medication. Or possibly, by now, my mind had learned to accept my coping strategy and could handle what had gone on years before. It had done what it always did—squashed everything I didn't want to face at the time into that "I'll deal with it later" box.

Anyway, I was in the middle of telling the group about some of my childhood experiences, when the therapist stopped me, mid-sentence.

She said, "Corinna, you are telling me something like this, and yet you are smiling. It's as if you're telling someone else's story."

It was only when she mentioned it that I realised for myself, and for the first time, that I was showing no emotion. I was completely detached.

That detachment was something I never really saw as a repeat occurrence or unconscious reaction to how mum had treated me, until recently. Until I was gathering my thoughts and the material for this book in fact.

My coaching technique now takes the client back as far and in as little time as possible to remove the emotions. There's no call for prolonged chatting and dragging up the past.

I often wish I'd known about these techniques sooner. But, as this was part of my journey that I had to take, would I be the catalyst for so many positive changes and transformations in others if I had?

Chapter 7

Holding On To The True You

I've already mentioned I used to suffer from Tonsillitis, but by this time I had also started to experience a severe back problem. When it first started, it was just the lower part of my spine, causing Sciatica. Then gradually, my knees and legs were affected. And now, my upper spine and ribs.

Constant pain drives through me every day. Physical pain is just a way of life, and I've learned to live with it.

But I remember when it started back in 2004. I had this stiffness and twinge in my lower back. As I walked down the stairs one particular morning, my legs suddenly gave way. Just as something crumbles if it can't hold the weight it's carrying.

I was bed bound for three weeks and was prescribed extremely strong painkillers.

This same sudden attack of pain started to happen every so often, and I'd have to be careful not to ignore it, as the GP didn't know what was actually going on, or what it might lead to.

I adapted my life as best I could. But eventually, in 2009, it was the severity of the pain that forced me to give up my job as cabin crew, which I absolutely loved.

If you've read any of my other books, or simply noticed the title of this one, you can probably gather that travelling was my dream. So when I was grounded by my pain, I wanted to stay connected and became a travel agent.

A year into the new job, I had been doing really well.

I can remember telling grandad when he was in the hospital that I was loving it, smashing all my sales targets, and feeling part of a team again.

He loved the fact that I was back on the ground and, in his opinion, safe. He never did like me flying, and worried about me every day. Mind you, he made me laugh telling me he once had a dream that I would take over from the pilot one day, land in the back garden, and pop in for a cup of tea!

But, being as close as we were, he could also see through the smiles and knew it wasn't the same buzz I used to have up in the air. He knew how much I loved that job, so no matter how much it scared him and my nan, and although he'd never put too much pressure on me to do anything else, he was definitely happier with me being grounded.

Anyway, back to the travel agency, as you know, grandad's passing and breaking up with my ex-fiancé had taken their toll on me, and things had started to slip.

A few months later, we started to hear the rumours, and feel the uneasiness, of looming redundancies. There were two of our stores very close to each other, and it was our store that was closing down within a week. This horrendous, uncomfortable tension began to grow in the office very quickly.

The girls were all young, and they had it in them to keep fighting for any sales that came in.

They went from being friendly 'team players' to scrapping over the slightest hint of a potential customer sale. It felt like I was back at school. Only I never even used to play games when I was in the playground, so I certainly wasn't going to do it here.

I said in the introduction how certain scents and situations can bring back recollections from your past. Well, at this time there were so many memories flooding back to my conscious awareness.

That playhouse kitchen moment started haunting me once again.

And the memory of that hot summer day walking home from school when I was attacked by the bullies.

I knew I was about to be pushed out, pushed to one side. Again.

This time, though, even though there was much more riding on my job, I had no spark or strength left in me, to stand up against the insecure office bully, or the bureaucracy of the corporate world.

I had already taken a massive pay cut to work there when I gave up my eight-year career as cabin crew. And as I was one of the last ones in, I knew I was likely to be one of the first to be cut—either with or without a 'package'.

I had to do something. I just couldn't work out what.

Where was my grandad now? Where was my £5 at the school gate or by the local shop where he would wait for me to come out at lunchtime? I needed him to talk sense and make me see I was strong enough.

"Come on Corinna, you're a Stringer! You're better than this."

Without him now, though, I felt lost and lonely.

I built up the courage to go back in after another couple of days off sick.

With my resignation letter in one envelope and the acceptance of redundancy in another, (as nan would say, "It's worth asking, you never know!") I asked my manager whether there was any likelihood of redundancy. When I was told bluntly "No," I handed over the resignation letter.

My sales had been going down. I had no interest in being there. And, unsurprisingly, they made no attempt to keep hold of me.

Much as I knew that I'd pretty much manifested this moment, by repeatedly signalling to the Universe that I didn't want to be there, the reality still hurt.

I'd let myself down, and I knew I'd let my grandad down too.

Would he understand why I was feeling so low, and felt incapable of pulling myself together?

Depression wasn't ever really a thing for the older generation. My nan's voice kept coming up, reminding me "that's life, my lovely. It'll all come out in the wash. You just have to get on with it."

As I mentioned earlier, I learned a lot about building a business, and being in business from my grandparents. The resilience and power to make things work, even if those around you doubt you, and question your ability.

Yes, they taught me the value of money, and how to save money and make money.

But through my grandad, I also saw how people actually buy your personality and trust before they buy your product or service.

Travel was still in my veins even after resigning from the agents. So, the next best thing was to apply to an online travel company.

When I applied for the job, I imagined I would be smiling my way through my shifts, spending hours each day on calls, talking to excited customers about where they wanted to go. I knew enough about the booking systems and what was possible if you wanted to make it happen, so I looked forward to upgrading their flights and car hire, and creating the best packages I could for their dream family holidays.

Truth was, I absolutely hated it!

Without going into too much detail, the company was built on greed and dishonesty, which were very much against my values, and beyond a level of behaviour I could comprehend, let alone fulfil. It just didn't sit right with me at all. I couldn't take hard-earned money off these people like this.

Something I discovered in my own journey, and also what I teach my coaching clients today, is to live by your values. Understanding this is key. This practice alone is what forms the very basics of my own business, and has been a game changer for my clients in theirs.

So basically, I was travelling miles to work in a job that I hated. For a boss I couldn't stand. The money was worse than before. By now, I was in so much debt after taking a pay cut, that I was on the verge of losing my home.

I got to my desk one day, spectacularly late. I had no interest in being there. So, filled with everything other than enthusiasm, my meds were still zapping what little energy I could find, feeling that level of tiredness, I put on my headset.

I felt physically sick to the stomach. My heart was heavy, and I was back in that bubble of numbness that I couldn't get out of.

One call finished. The flights hadn't been available, so whilst the customer was still on hold my manager told me to package the holiday and sell it anyway. This was to build their excitement, only for me to then call them back later to either encourage them to upgrade, or the alternative was that their holiday would be cancelled.

The flights were never there in the first place, which I knew, and it made me feel sick that I was being asked to do such a thing. It was totally against my values.

I sat and stared around the open-plan sales floor at all the other agents. Tied to their desks with their headsets on, not one of them looked exactly overboard with excitement.

Are they in the same situation as me? Are they so desperate to make a living, that they're prepared to leave their pride and respect for other human beings at the door? Or do they actually enjoy what they're doing? That was all it took.

A few minutes later, I took a massive breath, pulled off my headset, picked up my bag, and stood up in what felt like one swift, powerful, movement.

The guy on the bank of desks next to me looked up at me, with a questioning look on his face.

"Do you know what?" I said. "I don't wanna be here anymore. In fact, I'm **not** gonna be here anymore."

"Where are you going?"

"I've no idea," I replied back. "But right at this minute, I've just got to go home."

I started walking away from my desk, turned the top half of my body from my hips slightly back, and waved to our boss. "Bye! That's me done. I'm not coming back!"

Muffled sounds began, along with an awkwardness of shuffling in seats, as people who had hardly ever heard me speak, let alone do something as brave (you can also read 'stupid' into this if you choose) as this, also pulled their headsets off, trying to work out what had just happened!

Now I look back (I mean, hindsight is a wonderful thing!), it was like one of those cringe-worthy Bridget Jones moments when she'd said or done something we, as the audience, thought was hilariously unbelievable. Yet there she was, strutting away from the scene, with such pride and force in her stride!

In my case, I'd only been working there for about three months, but as I walked out of that office (with trousers on, so at least I knew I wasn't having a Bridget Jones skirt in knickers moment!) for the very last time, I felt free. As free as I had ever been, and lighter than I'd felt in a long, long time.

Everything grandad had told me about building trust in your customers was flooding back to me. And I knew I'd done the right thing.

Until...

I got into my car, and had that 'holy s***' moment!

The inner voice kicked in again.

What have you just done? You've got bills to pay!

What about the mortgage? It's not going to sort itself out, you know.

How are you going to afford to live? How are you going to get another job?

It's surprising how many thoughts go through your head in such a short space of time!

You've heard the fight, flight, or freeze analogy?

Well, I fell right into an industrial-sized freezer!

This time, the car was the bubble I was once again trapped inside. I felt claustrophobic again. I couldn't see out of the windows.

I had all those feelings of fear. I was sweaty. I looked around to see if anyone was watching.

Should I go back? Could I go back? (Those bloody voices!)

NO WAY!

But maybe you should go back.

Do you really want to go back there? Even if you do, your sales will be crap. You hate it. It goes against everything you believe. What they do, it's just not right.

So, what are you going to do instead?

I knew I'd burned those bridges well and truly to the ground. There was no going back.

Remember, by now I was close to losing my house. My income was already inconsistent. So I needed to find something secure, and guaranteed, to pay the bills.

Yes, the panic hit for a short time. But do you know what? It felt somehow comforting.

Was it panic, then? Or was it a hint of excitement? Maybe neither. Maybe I knew deep down that what I'd done was right.

I didn't ever go back there again.

The first call I made was to a friend who owned a cleaning business I'd already been doing a few hours each week. But the hours she could give were nowhere near what I needed to even clear the bills, let alone to live!

Freeze mode soon went. Next was 'survival' mode. That survival mode I'd often had, even as a child, fending for myself when mum disappeared for days.

When something happens that doesn't go the way you want, there's no point wallowing in self-pity (I know this now). You just have to get on with it (and there she is again, good old nan!)

It was time to start something new. To *create* something new. And to be my own boss.

Now, I would never recommend that you just quit your job the way I did. But for me, it felt right. Yes, it was a huge risk. A risk I had to take, and it was worth it.

"Don't wait. The time will never be just right"- Napoleon Hill

YES!! This was just the start. I could feel my fight coming back!

Chapter 8

Tough Love

I'd like to give you the opportunity to pause for a minute and think.

What have you had your heart set on achieving for years, yet still haven't taken that leap?

Are you dreaming of writing a book? They say there's a story inside of all of us, you know.

Perhaps you have a passion for running – maybe a marathon? Or even competing in the Olympics?

Or maybe you want to start a business, or grow your business to the next level, so you can live your true vision and passion, and be happy every day?

I had put off writing this book for many years. Procrastination, now that's a funny thing too. And I'll come back to that later.

But the thing is, when I finally realised *why* I was writing it, the book came to life!

My WHY? To help change lives, and even save some lives in the process (which I literally have, just recently).

You see, this might be my story. But I'm sure that you will be able to relate to at least one point within it.

Just recently, my wonderful mentor and friend, Jessen James, reminded me about how our stories can become someone else's survival guide. Not that I needed external validation, but it reinforced my reasons for writing this book.

So allow me to continue and let you into a secret of how a path that was paved in failure, struggles, loss, lies, and deceit, helped me discover the true power of the mind.

****

Oh, as a bit of an aside, I've not yet mentioned him, so you might wonder where my dad fitted into my life. Well, sadly, he didn't.... he was an alcoholic.

From me being very young, mum decided the best thing for him was to leave him to his own devices. If he was going to drink himself to an early grave, then so be it. But it wasn't her job to try and "fix him".

The thing I've learned though is that nobody is actually ever broken.

We don't need fixing. Sometimes, we simply need a helping hand, a mentor, or a spiritual guide.

Whatever you want to call it, mum wasn't prepared to be that person for him. When she found out he had cancer, she broke it to me by saying, "We'll know when your dad has died because all the pubs will go out of business."

So, I never knew much about my dad. I realise now that she thought she was doing the right thing, certainly by shielding me from the sights she didn't ever want me to see.

But before my inner work and mind studies, I didn't understand her approach. All I knew was I never wanted to do the same to anyone.

****

I'd kept hearing about this dating app from different people. And although I'd always laughed off the fact that I was single, and ignored the 'encouragement' from the girls in the office, fooling myself that I was fine on my own (*why would I need anyone to ruin my quiet nights in anyway?*) was getting a little bit boring.

So, when I finally got fed up with them going on about me joining this app, I figured one night when I was home alone, with nothing else to do, I might as well give it a go. Just a quick look won't do any harm.

I know, you're smiling right now. Even I am as I write. I mean, this can only end badly, right?

And yes. It soon became like an addiction.

I am blessed to be able to say that by this point, much of the old me had gone.

Now, I was an older version. A young woman whose inner strength may have waned, but there were glints of my outer confidence coming back. I'd learned how to paint on a smile and give the air of grace and dignity from my days flying high as cabin crew.

So, yes, on the outside, it probably looked as though I could flirt with the best of them!

Notice I said "outer confidence" though. Because, in truth, after a while of playing the dating game, it wasn't me being me.

I wasn't me anymore at all in fact.

Life was so far from where it had been. I was different. And extremely fragile.

Still, I tried. I'd had a few dates, and it served me well, like a distraction from what had gone on before. It was getting me back in the saddle again, so to speak.

Another huge lesson in life is to go with your gut instinct.

You know, your gut instinct, like every emotion we feel, is there for a reason. We sense excitement when we know something feels right. I know I start to feel hot and sweaty, even though I'm not sweating (too much information? Sorry!) Then I get this floaty feeling of being free.

If something feels completely out of alignment though, I have this sickly feeling. I've never physically been sick, no matter how much I've known something isn't right. It's just an overwhelming feeling.

I have no doubt some of you are nodding right now— you know what I mean, don't you?

Funny also how we always call it a 'gut instinct' even if we feel it somewhere different. My gut instinct, or sickly feeling, is more in my chest than in my stomach.

One thing is the same for us all though. Our body can tell us what our mind cannot. We can try all we like to override what our body senses tell us. But the body is always right.

My gut instinct has never been wrong.

So, when this situation came up in a particular relationship, and I knew I had to make a choice between:

1. keeping quiet about something I'd found out, that had made me feel really uneasy, and staying in the relationship;
2. ending the relationship and walking away without helping him; or
3. ending the relationship on the understanding I would help him.

I let my gut instinct make that choice.

How many times have you had a gut feel about something, done the opposite, and then wished you'd trusted your instinct in the first place?

I'm not going into detail about the situation, other than to say, I am so pleased I trusted my gut and followed what it was telling me to do.

Everything worked out perfectly for us both. We broke up, but when I saw him about six months later, he had completely turned his life around. He actually told me he was grateful for my faith in him, and his actions proved that.

There are always lessons to be learned. Even if you do decide to intentionally go against your intuition or instinct, the Universe will find a way of delivering something to show you what you *should* have done!

I'll talk more later about how I work with my gut feel in both relationships and business.

But I'll leave you with more words of wisdom from my nan, which I am sure many of you may already swear by:

"The Lord will never give you anything more than you can handle."

So, even when the road ahead looks bleak. Or you come up against something you cannot see a way around or through, over or under. Ask your body, and your heart, to show you the way.

Whatever comes up for you, it will be a lesson—good, bad, or indifferent!

Chapter 9

Nothing Changes, if Nothing Changes

When I hit my teens, I had started to take more note of what my nan and grandad, and I guess my mum too, were showing me. Not just in the way they spoke to me, each other, and everyone around them. But also in their actions, reactions, and general behaviours. I was led to believe that people should be strong, and not show any signs of weakness.

So when I was hit with 'The Black Box' (which became my name for depression), I was so ashamed to tell anyone, especially my nan and grandad.

The irony of the reference being associated with an aircraft black box recorder has not been lost on me. You might have heard of the black box being searched for after an air accident, as it is where all the vital information is stored from that particular aircraft's flights. It enables the accident investigators to pull together the exact stages of the fault, fire, or whatever it was that caused the accident.

You will read later how the information (or the story) from my life is what led to my depression, and how each piece within my black box has then given me all the information I needed to write this book, realise my goals, and become the coach and speaker that I am today.

The only option I had was to go it alone.

It was unlike me to *choose* to give up on anything. I started looking back at situations and experiences in my life. I became intrigued about human psychology and wanted to gain more of an understanding of how the mind works. It seems that sometimes our minds work in a positive way. And other times, playing tricks on us, and testing our limits!

I also finally acknowledged that there had actually been a big problem for years, when I was diagnosed with depression. And right then, I knew I had to find a solution.

I no longer wanted to keep going around in circles. Taking one step forward and two steps back. Feeling miserable, like a failure, and a burden to anyone who was interested. I kept thinking back to that Christmas Day and how I'd been found on the floor after my overdose.

I never wanted that for me. Nor for anyone to find me that way again, or even worse.

What I did want though, it's just as important, incidentally, to know what you do and don't want from life, was to make my nan and grandad proud of me. I wanted to know that they would always be smiling for me, no matter where they were.

Back then, when people talked about anything to do with mental health, there was this awful stigma about being 'crazy.' I might have often *felt* crazy, but I wasn't ready to come out in the open and tell people I actually was!

Nor did I want to admit to being depressed. I had *no right* to be depressed. There were people with far worse problems than mine.

I should be a strong, independent character. I should be able to cope with this (inner voices again). But the truth was, I couldn't.

And as a result of the shame and embarrassment, it's taken me six years to start telling people my story.

I'd had a complete breakdown. Being admitted for daily treatment and assessment as an out-patient at the local hospital wasn't the best time. But it was a step towards acceptance, and managing the healing process.

So, back to the time of the diagnosis and treatment, what also came with that was a heck of a lot of stark realisations. Thankfully, I allowed myself to be open to learning from them, and taking whatever action I needed to take.

It's quite scary, when you're in the thick of something like that, you really can't see how bad it is. It's only when you do finally reach out to the experts, someone who might understand what it's like to go through it, or at least have an idea of what treatment is needed, that the truth starts to surface.

As the chapter heading suggests, "**Nothing changes, if nothing changes.**"

That's another phrase that has stood firm in my mind for years.

It sounds so obvious, but how many times do we have to do the same thing, before finally accepting that the answer is always going to be the same too? See, my explanation is much easier to handle than Einstein's (definition of insanity)!

So, the first, and most important 'aha' moment in my acceptance of The Black Box, was realising that, if I don't change, then nobody is going to help me. I simply had to change. I must start asking for help.

The second, was that there **had to be** a positive to come out of this negative situation. Even if I couldn't see it at the time.

"Find a place inside where there's joy, and the joy will burn out the pain."
- Joseph Campbell

Chapter 10

Fear, Strength, and Forgiveness

Following my exit from the call centre, I started to get some of my Stringer 'survivor' strength back.

I mentioned earlier that I had been working for a friend in her cleaning company to earn a bit of extra cash. Well, initially when I asked her for more work, the figures didn't add up.

Nan had always drilled it into me, "You've got to earn your own keep, girl."

She and grandad both taught me to be resourceful. So I looked through everything I had, could I sell stuff? Can I get bar work? I had years of experience in customer service, and that was huge at the time. Surely something would turn up.

I was prepared to do pretty much anything (within reason!) to make money.

Anyway, my friend came back to me not so long after that first call, when one of her cleaning ladies went on

Maternity Leave (see, I always knew something would come up!) And that was the start of work flooding in. Remember also that I was on the brink of losing my house. Plus, I wanted distractions to help take my mind off everything happening to me. I say everything was happening "to" me because I was still in that mindset of blaming everything and everybody else.

I hadn't been in control, but this was the turning point for me.

My hours increased. I was covering for other people, left, right, and centre. And I loved it!

The irony wasn't lost on me that when mum used to go out sometimes for days at a time, and I was left home alone, cleaning became my coping mechanism. I developed OCD. It was my therapy. Here I was, doing literally hundreds of hours of cleaning work, and it was helping ease my anxiety-driven OCD once again. Only this time I was earning a crucial income for it, and it was helping reduce my OCD in a completely different way.

It was daft things like, deliberately not washing my hands before eating my sandwiches. I was making conscious choices to go against my OCD, and it was working. I'd put myself in positions where I changed my pattern of behaviour. After all, I had cleaning products all over me, why did I need to wash my hands so often? Why did I need to wipe my hands before I touched my steering wheel when they were already as clean as they could possibly be?

It soon became one of those unconscious things I referred to in the Introduction. I stopped the routine that had gone on for years, so my unconscious mind started to believe I didn't need to do it. And it allowed me to replace the compulsive behaviour with other, more constructive focal points and activities that I learned so much more from—learning about ME.

The job change had also brought a lifestyle change, and although the OCD hasn't gone altogether, I am far much more in control of the old habits. I can step in before they take over.

In my book, "The Art of Feeling Fear and Taking Back Control", I mention talking to my nan and mum one Christmas about how things were going. Nan especially, could see how many hours I was working - days, nights, and any time that was needed - I was proud of what I was achieving. I had the energy to work, and it was going really well.

But her wording made me stop and think. She still referred to it as a "job" and not a business. Maybe that was how the older generation viewed all work. Did she mean to point out that it was, in my eyes, just a job? That I was employed by someone else. It doesn't really matter, because of course this is how I saw things that were said to me. I took it more literally and more personally.

I just saw it as another sign of me being a failure.

Yes, I had the flexibility to get the work done in my time, on my terms, and with a level of freedom. And, although I was already earning enough to warrant an Accountant (yes, I saw paying taxes a massive positive!), the cleaning company wasn't my own business.

Another huge realisation struck that I had been so desperate to earn an income, consistent enough to be able to pay the mortgage, keep the house, pay the bills, and everything that came with being an adult, that I'd taken anything and everything I could. What was *available* to me. **Not** what I was worthy of.

"Never allow yourself to be so desperate, that you end up settling for far less than you deserve"

And I soon felt the brunt of that reality when I was pushed to one side yet again.

However the conversation off to the side may have started, the outcome was me being put down and pushed IN FRONT OF A CUSTOMER (yes folks, that is in big shouty letters, because it was so humiliating!) This was the ultimate display of rudeness and a complete lack of respect for me, and the customer.

I had worked too bloody hard for this. I'd given my all for her company, and built up a huge client base for her.

What was I doing, leaving myself open to this kind of s*&t? (note the inner voice taking me into victim mentality mode once again).

She'd become bitter over the smallest of things, and because of the way we'd set up our working 'arrangement', I didn't really have a leg to stand on.

Even my nan was surprised at the way my so-called friend had behaved. And being an east end girl, my nan had seen some ruthless businesswomen in her time!

It took me about two years after walking out of the travel industry altogether, to finally establish myself as a business owner. Multiple businesses, in fact.

I saw the massive potential in commercial and domestic cleaning, so I set up a cleaning company of my own. But that wasn't enough for me. I used to sit up for hours on end working out how to create and build websites (which was a new concept and a massive novelty back then), so I managed to save myself a fortune, as well as bring in additional income from that. And I even passed a Pet First Aid course, so I could add pet sitting to my transferable skills! I truly diversified!

I was mixing with successful business owners, millionaires, and multi-business entrepreneurs. Surrounded by nice cars, and a lavish champagne lifestyle. That wasn't for me and I would never fit in with the flash city party goers (it made me think too much about mum's canapes and cocktails!) For once, I didn't mind being on the sidelines. But my life was amazing even so.

A few men came and went. More went, than stayed, which was possibly a good thing! All that seemed to be happening was I kept attracting the wrong type. Again, and again.

One of them became overly obsessed. He wanted me available constantly to take any of his calls or reply to emails, messages, etc at random times. He hated me networking with any of the 'rich and famous,' as he saw them.

I know he thought I was up to no good, but I'm not like that at all. He assumed I would leave him for one of the guys I'd met through business forums and social events. I couldn't get my head around this. I wasn't anywhere near their radar, let alone on it. And even if I was, I wasn't in the slightest bit interested. They were business associates. I was so laser focused on making something of myself, and I wouldn't risk anything for my businesses back then.

Anyway, of course the attention was lovely at first. I had come across some strange guys during my 'getting back in the saddle' phase, and it was nice to know someone had my back and seemed to genuinely care about me.

Whenever I was going out, I had to let him know what time I'd be back so he could check in and make sure I was safe. If I ever forgot, or just fell asleep when I got home, without contacting him, he took it personally.

At first I thought it was quite cute. But it soon became uncomfortable, and he'd actually turn angry.

He started getting a little bit more physically manipulative too. I could handle most of what he did to me. Although I knew it wasn't exactly nice.

One particular time I was out though, he did his usual ritual of making sure (repeatedly) that he knew where I was and who I was with – whether he liked the answer or not.

I'd missed a couple of his calls during the evening, and when I eventually spoke to him, he turned really aggressive. I couldn't quite believe what I was hearing.

He basically threatened to throw my cats, computer, and all my personal possessions out of the window. Then said he was going to burn down my rental property, which was bringing in a lot of money at that time. He wanted to ruin my life.

I was simply out with some entrepreneur connections. Some had become really good friends that I could confide in and assured me everything would be okay. That's the thing with having a great community around you. It's not just work, it's a lifestyle. So, I stayed out. He was *not* going to control me anymore.

Even though inside I felt fearful, I hoped deep down that it was all just talk, and some kind of weird bravado, to get my attention.

When I got back into the flat, it was dark.

That uneasy gut feeling was with me again. Something wasn't as it should be.

As I walked further into the room, and switched on the lights, he came out of the bedroom, and launched himself at me... with a hammer.

I guess I had enough of his behaviour and the whole situation by that point. Maybe I was expecting a showdown. Had I already prepared myself, and subconsciously gone into "fight" mode?

Because, without hesitation, I screamed at him, "Well come on then! DO IT!"

Surprised at my own strength, and courage, I'd managed to dial 999 without him knowing. I kept him talking, trying to calm him down. Thankfully, I saw that nothing had actually been moved or broken in any way. His threats had been empty. But it dawned on me in those few moments that I had been living on my nerves for I don't know how long.

The Police arrived and after an initial discussion, taking a few notes, but not really paying all that much attention to what I was saying, they took him downstairs, and out to their car.

It wasn't the kind of conversation I'd been expecting. It all seemed a bit too relaxed to make me feel safe and comforted by their actions.

Now, I'm not exactly tall. And I was certainly never going to be able to defend myself against someone like him if I was taken by complete surprise in the future. But they did NOTHING!

I could see from the window that they were all out there sitting chatting away. *Are they laughing? Are they laughing at me?*

I already felt belittled enough as it was. This was an absolute kick in the teeth for me.

I just sat in the bedroom and waited for him to come back in. Which he did. Full of apologies—as empty as his threats. But he didn't stop at that.

He told me never to call the Police again. There'd be no point because he knew loads of the local coppers, and would always get let off with nothing more than a quick "naughty boy" comment. As he was telling me this, he was smirking and pointing his finger right in my face. You know that really sly kind of smirk? And so close to my face, I could feel the spit hitting my cheek as he spoke.

I felt physically sick.

The outcome? Not even a caution. His aggressive behaviour. His physical and verbal threats. They were considered not serious enough to take any further. I wouldn't be surprised if it wasn't even ever recorded.

We stayed together, for no other reason than by this time he owed me a lot of money (*how did I always end up like this?*)

Walking out, as I'd done so recklessly from the call centre, wasn't an option this time. I was living with this guy and there were long-term tenants in my rental property, so I couldn't go there.

And one more reason I couldn't leave there and then...

I was pregnant.

Throughout the pregnancy, he had pulled me by my hair, told me over and over that he didn't believe the baby was his, and was physically and verbally aggressive towards me too.

I ended up in hospital three times and feared for not only myself, but for my baby. The last time I was in hospital, I signalled to the nurses that I needed to be seen whilst he was outside smoking. They took no notice and I was in too much pain to make a fuss.

Finally, I got into the treatment room, just about to open up about what had been happening, when he burst in. So, once again, I went home without saying a word.

Those of you who know me, know I have no children, so the pregnancy did not turn out as I had hoped it would. Not all directly to do with him, and perhaps it was for the best in the long run.

So, I didn't walk out at that time, but I did make a plan.

And my cunning plan worked. It took grit and determination from me, and more hateful mental and physical bullying from him in the meantime, but I knew I would get out eventually.

I cut back on socialising, sold a few bits and pieces, and took on more cleaning jobs. I soon learned to hide the sickly sensation and flinches whenever he came near me. But I wheedled everything possible out of him for the next four months.

I finally got all the money back that he owed me, and built up enough in hidden savings, so I could leave.

The same pattern of hounding, harassment, and hurtful messages, social media comments, and vile attention-seeking behaviour continued even after I'd gone.

A restraining order didn't stop him. The police claimed they hadn't been able to find him (even though I gave them all the information they were likely to need).

He must have bored himself in the end, and moved onto some other poor, unsuspecting female. Because eventually, the contact fizzled out. The case was closed, but the fear was still there for me.

I saw him from a distance a couple of years later.

Luckily, he didn't see me, or I don't think he did.

I, on the other hand, was frozen to my seat. Those same feelings of fear, shame, and disgust reappeared, even though I hadn't seen him for a long time. The ones I thought had been buried away. But no, my unconscious mind kicked in and brought them all back.

By that time, I was seeing a lovely guy who was working on one of our construction sites not far from the pub where I was at that moment. I'd got some work to do after the meeting I'd had earlier that morning, so I decided to stay there. I was so engrossed in what I was doing, that it was only when I lifted my head for a breather that I noticed **he** was sitting over the other side of the bar area.

I called my partner and asked him to come over. As I said, I'm not big, so he shielded me as I packed up my bits from the table, and we walked out.

It was a precious thing to feel safe, even in the face of that evil man.

Chapter 11

Time to Heal

"Time, and the power of the mind, are great healers."

This is what I teach my clients.

My videos, broadcasts, and coaching always come from the heart. The fruit of my real-life experiences.

Because sometimes when we are in this state of denial and low self-worth, it's hard to relate to people who seem to have 'all their shit together.'

I want people who hear me speak, read my books, or join my coaching programmes, to know I haven't always been in the place I am now. And I'm okay with that.

It can be quite off-putting, actually, if you believe the person you are being mentored by, or the one guiding you through your tough times, is perfect! So, it's nice to know that 'stuff' happens to us all, and it's that stuff that makes us who we are.

I am so grateful to the few people that pulled me back from the edge without even knowing it. That's why I keep interlacing references to my mum.

I remember saying to a very dear friend of mine "I just can't cope with all of this anymore. I just can't."

His response came straight back at me without a single hint of doubt,

"Yes, you can! You can deal with anything. You're Corinna. Remember what your grandad used to say? You're a Stringer. We are stronger than that."

At the time I remember thinking, *"What the hell was that supposed to mean anymore?"*

But now I can see it so clearly.

He believed in me. He had faith in me. Even in my darkest moments. He knew my strengths, and my weaknesses. And he knew this was just a bump on my runway.

What about your experiences?

Take a moment to think about who always has faith in you, even when you feel you no longer have faith in yourself.

Do you recognise and thank them for it? Or do you simply take it for granted?

What instances can you recall now where they have shown you their support?

••

I had to reach for those kind words over, and over, again, even though they seemed to mean nothing, or at least not make much sense to me, at the time they were said.

Now I know they actually meant a great deal.

Having the faith and slowly starting to believe that I could get through it, I focused on one small step at a time. Every. Single. Day.

I still to this moment think of those words if ever I feel that I can't do something. I thought of them many times whilst writing this book. My grandad's way of still being with me, I guess.

He would want me to be heard. He would be proud of me for stepping up and no longer keeping these dark days hidden. Not to show off about how much I have managed to achieve.

But he knows that this book will ring true with at least one or two of you lovely readers.

So coming out in the open with the good, the bad, and the ugly experiences is worth every memory that crops up as I write.

I don't think many people really understood what was happening back then. And to be honest, I didn't want anyone to know. I wore a mask. A mask that you, yourself, might be wearing right now?

It took years to accept that we simply have to come across some people and go through certain situations to form our lives. Some of them stay (some longer than they are welcome!)

Remember, too, that some people come into your life as mere lessons. Others are blessings. Some stay and some go.

They may have their own reasons, and we are not supposed to know these reasons straight away.

What would life be like if we all had a straight path to our dream destination? What would it feel like to go sailing through life without the challenges we have to face, before we totally get it?!

It's going through these moments that help create the individuals we are, teach us gratitude for the people who have come into our lives as a blessing, and enable us to reach our destiny.

But it saddens me to think that some people can hurt us so easily. Sometimes by leaving us. Sometimes, it's the things they do or say to us, and quite often through no fault of their own. As I mentioned earlier, people are not their behaviour, which is something I open the way for my clients to understand as we work through conscious and subconscious beliefs and behaviours.

They know no different. Especially if they have seen and felt the same themselves. Those conditioned behaviours that are drilled into us, remember? They could be anything. From the most caring and honest reactions, to the most bitter, spiteful, and condescending comments.

There is no excuse for behaving this way, but at least it gives some explanation as to why some *can*, and *choose to*, hurt us intentionally. Every behaviour has a positive intention, despite how it may feel for us at the time.

I was yet to discover this during my healing process. And when I did, it all made sense.

****

During all the ups and downs in 2015, one day I was researching how to promote my cleaning business online. We were doing well from referrals, but it's only so long before you have to move your attention to new avenues for marketing. That's another crucial lesson in business, by the way. Customer testimonials and word of mouth are amazing, but don't sit back and expect them to do all the work for you!

Anyway, around that time, an old school friend of mine popped up in a video for a new advertising business which meant you could make money advertising other people's businesses. So I contacted her to see what it was all about.

Running a business can be a lonely place. Particularly with little or no support from your loved ones. So it was great to be out there with a whole new circle of budding, buzzing, and energy-building entrepreneurs.

When it comes to my own values, and those of my business, I appreciate and totally advocate collaboration over competition. It's something I learned many years ago, and have continued to encourage in my clients today.

My confidence grew as I got more and more involved with this business. I started to run my own presentations and bring others from all around Essex and the southeast to set up their own businesses, too. I learned a lot, very quickly, about network marketing, and even more about effectively promoting businesses. I threw myself 100% into my own businesses, and used my business experience to help those in the teams I was building.

I also met many influential and character-building mentors in the public speaking world, which was something even then that I knew I wanted to pursue.

A very important piece of advice here is that you never know who might be watching you when you put yourself out there, or even just going about your day-to-day life. Even though the people you are with at the time might not be able to help you, others who are in their circles might. And door after door can open up for you if you are willing to take a chance.

It seemed that these points were all coming true for me in a very short space of time!

The MLM business earnings and promotions enabled me to travel with them throughout Europe, New Zealand, Australia, and Bali, which of course felt like I was living my dream again.

I was up on stage, presenting in front of hundreds of people just like me hoping to make their millions.

And the best part of it was the income I was generating from doing what I loved.

I'd wanted to travel all my life, but had been put off by my mum telling me if I went off around the world straight from school, I'd never be able to find a job when I got back if I didn't have any qualifications. They used to worry so much (only I saw it as nagging and it really annoyed me at the time). At every opportunity, mum would try and hold me back or put me down.

A memory cropped up just as I was writing this section, of when I was around five or six years old, and I loved my ballet classes. Isn't it something all little girls dream of? Well, my dream lasted only a short time. No sooner had I been looking forward to every class, feeling every bit the little prima ballerina, then the classes came to an abrupt halt.

Mum told me the ballet school had closed down suddenly. Strange then, that years later as I was driving by that same building, I saw some young girls coming out dressed in their beautiful pastel pink leggings, hair tied up perfectly in a bun.

I mentioned it to mum. The answer came like a knife in my heart. "Oh, it didn't close down. You just weren't good enough."

Remember that the majority of our beliefs, our core beliefs and limiting beliefs, are created before the age of seven. This feeling of not being good enough was something that would continue to be instilled in my heart and in my head for many years to come.

So yes, she'd be proud of me in front of friends and family. And then, even when I was succeeding as a cabin crew member, she'd call me a 'glorified waitress in the sky' in private.

Travel was the reason I joined the airlines and loved the perks of being cabin crew. Many unsociable hours, away from home a lot, but the places we saw were amazing.

Things were different back then. I'm so pleased it has changed now and young people are learning from the world and life experiences, not just the school system.

Anyway, around the time I decided to pack my bags and leave that guy, I had the opportunity and the money to take an extended holiday in Australia, Bali, and ending in Dubai.

Suddenly, everything I had been through made sense. They had pointed me towards this direction, not my final destination, but life was bearable again.

In fact, I was feeling so positive again, the world was my oyster (or "lobster" as Vicky Pattison referred to in a recent guest podcast! It really made me giggle, as it's one of the things I would probably say).

Although many friends and business associates told me I was crazy to go off travelling alone, I was looking forward to it. A whole year away from everything and everybody I needed to recover from.

It was the perfect opportunity to reflect. Time to rebuild my visions and goals. And time to heal.

I read a lot while I was away. I learned a lot about myself in the process. And in addition to the knowledge I had picked up after my anxiety and depression diagnosis, I started to find the workings of the mind even more fascinating.

As was my usual style, I tried to stay away from anywhere 'normal' where the tourists would be hanging out. So during my stay in Bali I found the most beautiful place to hide away and restore my energy, far off the beaten track and way up in the mountains.

Something kept tugging away at me (the inner voices for once giving me a nudge in the *right* direction!) to go for a late night swim, and as I rolled over onto my back in the perfectly warm, still water, I looked up to see the most amazing patterns and star formations across the night sky.

I'm not saying there was necessarily anything different about the sky on this particular night. Just that I had probably never taken the time to notice it before. Certainly not with such a clear mind, anyway.

This might sound a bit cliché, but it was like I had been baptised—a feeling of cleanliness, as the water was so gently lapping around me and over my forehead. And a sense of love and protection surrounded me.

I'd also not noticed the illumination from the stars, the moon, and the lights from the complex before. But this particular night they bobbed up and down each time I took another stroke through the pool. I was experiencing my own psychedelic light show on water!

This night was the most memorable – my rebirth. The start of my new life.

From then on, everything I read helped me to answer so many outstanding questions from my childhood. I started to be able to make sense of the events and experiences I'd never understood. And although I had lost the advertising business and a lot of money with it, I kept pushing through.

By the time I went to Dubai towards the end of the year, I had renewed energy, and the desire to completely **rebuild** my life.

Chapter 12

A Different Kind of Pill

Now, I know depression and anxiety are never the same from one person to the next.

I've always hated taking pills for anything, so taking antidepressants for months on end, which left me feeling so lethargic all the time, was not my ideal solution.

If you're putting that many chemicals into your body, what must these be doing to your health? That's just my opinion, by the way.

But, I did feel that the medication and medical treatment I was receiving was very generic. Please be assured that I blame nothing and nobody for this, and I was grateful to receive any help at all.

For me, though, I needed more.

I had to find something else.

What I eventually found was amazing!

And the more I found, the more amazing it was!

This became like a new addiction, far healthier than alcohol! I realised I was wanting to get up out of bed every morning. Even if I had been at an event or on a course which meant travelling back late the night before.

I gradually began to notice that the brain fog was lifting. I was thinking so much more clearly and making sensible decisions. I was slowly finding my purpose again.

I also know that as soon as I started to understand myself, my behaviours, and unravel my past, the mental clarity I found meant I no longer needed the same medication.

Self-development had become, for me, a perfect prescription – a different kind of pill.

Chapter 13

Abort, Divert, or Stay on My Flightpath?

You think that was the end of the struggle?

Typical of the way things had been going in my life (you have to admit, there were plenty of trends and patterns emerging!) It was when I returned from the 'healing' holiday that I learned the MLM business had collapsed.

Seriously? You couldn't make this stuff up!

Yes, it was a pyramid scheme (but then, many businesses are built in a pyramid structure. Well, that was what we'd been encouraged to confidently go back with if anyone ever questioned it) and the lucky fella at the top took all the money and disappeared. Not great!

So, if you are reading this right now, or you are hearing me talk about some of my life's misadventures from a stage presentation or a podcast, I'm sharing them with you now that I've worked through the feeling sorry for myself phase, and to enable you to see that everything is overcome-able (a new word I've created as I have rediscovered my inner strength and belief in myself).

Remember, I'm here now to talk you through *my* mistakes, to help create *your* power. To share how my *mess* has become my *message*!

You'll find out more about my messages by the way, and what you can learn from them, when you reach the end of this phase of my story.

For now though, returning from my holiday in the November of that year, I saw it as a whole new start. It didn't quite turn out the way I'd hoped (in fact, it didn't start the way I had envisaged it either!) But it was a fresh start nonetheless!

I wasn't going to let a fundamental flaw in my business dreams stop me, and I even met a new boyfriend on Christmas Eve too (I'm beginning to think maybe I am Bridget Jones!) Life was looking up for us both.

Maybe this slightly forced diversion away from the dream of the advertising millionaire-maker flightpath wasn't going to be so bad after all.

After a wonderful six months, we decided to move into a house together. We signed a two-year tenancy agreement, on the understanding with the landlady that during the two years, we would refurbish and redecorate the house.

On paper, it was absolutely perfect for us. We moved in with such excitement and enthusiasm!

Something was never quite right about the place though. And it's when we put so much pressure on ourselves to reach perfection, that when things throw us off track, it feels like a much harder pill to swallow.

We couldn't put our finger on what it was, it just seemed that luck never came our way whilst we were in there. Yes, we were so happy together, and had so many things in common. We had a mutual business drive and determination. Because of the agreement we had on the house, we were actually starting to save a little bit of money, and didn't mind staying in more often than going out. And life really was fantastic most of the time. Perhaps we had become a little bit *too* comfortable with life, and you know there's no way that feeling can last! Around 10 months into the tenancy agreement, we were visited by a couple of guys wanting to take photos to market the property.

What the actual…. ????

We tried in vain to get hold of our landlady. We'd signed the contract in good faith, and had made massive improvements to the house and the garden already.

142

We'd spent a fortune on it. We dreamed of buying the place after the tenancy expired.

How could she do this to us?

The two of us fell into that victim mentality that isn't easy to get out of if you allow it to continue for too long. He constantly moaned about how much the world, and every single person in it, was against us. Of course, that wasn't strictly true, and it used to annoy me to hear it all the time.

I tried so hard to help him see that things would improve if he could just change his mindset.

I coach my clients now, that when you have completed a little bit of inner work, it's never a 'done once, done forever' kind of thing. New challenges will keep coming up, and you have to keep delving deeper before you are fully through all the root causes of your problems. Another level, another devil is one of the best ways of putting it.

This wasn't the first big problem we'd faced together. But, it was the first time my own inner work had been challenged since the healing holiday.

There are times in life when we have to make difficult choices. Even sacrificing what we love, for the greater good. We eventually parted ways as a couple, but we continued to work together for some time after our split as business partners.

As I said, he wasn't one to look on the bright side of life as much as I was, and much as I tried to encourage him to trust the process and trust this journey that we have to go on through life, he wasn't quite there just yet!

He took a lot for granted, and spent time moaning about the most ridiculous things. In fact, if I'm honest, we had both started acting as if we knew it all, too! We were a little arrogant in some ways. It just shows that you become the average of the people you are surrounded by, so I'll give him the credit for changing me! He'll laugh at that bit if he reads this!

Of course, in the midst of it all, I didn't see it so clearly as I did as soon as I'd put two and two together.

I've learned more, particularly as I've developed different coaching modalities, about the energy and vibration needed to keep things on a positive trajectory. But we were so engrossed in our own little 'loved-up' world, content to stay in every night to save money, and spending all our spare time refurbishing the house to our standards, we didn't stop for a moment to look close enough to home to spot any red flags or warning signs.

Anyway, we stopped paying our rent immediately, which totally went against everything I had been brought up to believe. I was feeling different now though. I was fuming, and being surrounded by all this bitterness and negativity made me react differently to things I would usually dust off and ignore.

Our deposit had been paid in full upfront, so as we didn't expect to see any of that returned, we figured the heartless woman could take that into account to cover the additional time we stayed put. And then, when we thought we were about evens, we called it quits. We *were doing her a favour by leaving when we did, weren't we?! We could have dug our heels in and stayed there months after that!*

See what I mean about the arrogance? That's what we truly believed at the time though.

My vision (or my wish) from all those years ago had come true! I'd manifested myself into a state of homelessness!

You know by now this wasn't my first rodeo. It wasn't the first time I'd had to pack my bags and walk out of somewhere. Bonus this time though, it was only the property I was leaving, not the man as well!

He wanted us to find somewhere else together straight away, but there was no way we could do that. I had my cats, and a rock bottom credit rating. He had no money other than his business. Not exactly the best position to be in.

We decided it was best for him to go back to his nan's for a few months. Incidentally, she was called Jean, the same as my nan. Amazingly, we had both been raised by our nans, too.

So of course, the most reliable lady in my life wouldn't see me out on the streets.

Never one to let me down, my nan said I could move back there too. So, off I trundled once again, tail between my legs.

Me and my nan used to quarrel like you wouldn't believe! Two very strong-minded women having an argument was probably a sight to see. Much as she would eventually tell me "that's your opinion, this is mine, and I'm sticking to it", it was very rare that she would ever back down and say sorry, as such! This beautiful little twinkle would appear in her eye, and she'd give me a gentle nudge as if she knew I would forgive her for whatever tiny thing we had disagreed on in the first place. And that was considered the end of it.

I guess living with our nans helped us reassess our situation. To gain some perspective. And little did I know the favour would be returned not too far down the line.

The reason we created Jean Properties Ltd, which you'll find out more about, was because of our nans. They helped us to see life in a completely different light, to be grateful for all we had, and to push ourselves forward instead of sitting around moping and moaning!

I wanted to do something useful straight away. I couldn't wallow in what had happened, so I persuaded my partner to come with me as a volunteer at a local homeless shelter. I had hoped it might make him see the light—not literally turn to religion, but you know what I mean.

It was coming up to Christmas, and grateful that we weren't actually on the list of frequent visitors to the shelter, we were determined to do all we could to make life a little bit more pleasant for the ones who were. When you put yourself in a position like that, it's amazing what it does for your own sense of reality.

Perspective changes completely. We had started to consider ourselves as badly done to, poor souls who didn't deserve to be wronged. You know, wanting the sympathy vote all the time.

After the first visit, we sat in my car with the heating on, and I burst into tears.

"How can we complain?" I asked him. "We're going home to a warm bed tonight." It was bitterly cold outside, and we knew we would be taken care of by our nans.

We began to feel ashamed of how we saw our own lives. There were so many others far worse off than we were. And it was due to what we witnessed there, and what we experienced ourselves, whilst we were volunteering that we conceived our joint business idea.

He wanted to go into the property market, with a view to make places available for people like us who struggled to get onto the property ladder, or even to get any references to be able to rent. For people who were in a job transition, marriage or relationship breakdown, or other changes of circumstances. People who needed to move on and better their lives.

With my connections and business background, we knew this would work. And we had experienced it ourselves, so could appreciate what these people were struggling with.

My partner had been declared bankrupt previously. My credit rating, as I said, was rubbish. And we struggled to pull together the upfront payments for the last place.

Our ideal clients were those who were in that same place. Maybe divorcees, ex-forces, jobless or low paid people, or youngsters starting out in life. People, like me, who had pets and would rather sleep on the streets than to see their pets rehomed.

We knew we could make it work, and desperately wanted to help others. In fact, our tagline in the business is 'Let your future begin', and it is truly heart-led.

Anyway, some wonderful people visited that homeless shelter, and we soon became known to them all.

As I said, it was coming up to Christmas, so the weather really wasn't ideal for being out on the streets. Ironically, when I was sitting talking to people there one evening, it was a homeless guy who ended up making me a hot chocolate! I was supposed to be taking care of him. But they were all so grateful to have somewhere to get out of the wind and rain, even for a short time. You could see the joy on their faces at the fact that somebody took the time to talk to them, even just to notice them. It goes to show that sometimes it's the little things that we take for granted that can mean so much to others. The time you give to people, and the lives you can touch in this world, that really makes a difference. And so they loved handing out warm drinks, soup, and biscuits as much as we did. They felt needed. They had a purpose—something many of them had lived without for years.

One of the kind donations was a Christmas tree that could go outside the shelter. We were all busy decorating it when one of the guys we often saw coming in for a cuppa took out a handmade decoration from his pocket. It had been carefully wrapped, and clearly it had been lovingly created.

He started to tell me about a lady he had met many years ago in Paris, when he was a young man and travelled a lot. She had been special to him. But they lost touch, and when his circumstances changed, he knew he would never be able to go back to try and find her. Over the years, he had never forgotten her, and wanted this decoration to be something in her memory. It was the first time in many years that he'd had a Christmas tree to decorate, so this was even more special.

There was such a beautiful look in his eyes when he talked about his lady.

His story shook me up, and I'm not ashamed to admit there were tears. Thankfully, it was raining so he couldn't tell the tears from the raindrops! Once again ashamed, I couldn't cry, I had nothing to be sad about. *Corinna, pull yourself together!* I don't think I was sad for me, though. I think it was the harsh realisation that there were so many other people out there with things to feel sad about.

Whatever it was, I felt truly honoured to be able to share that emotional experience with him. And it made me even more determined to help those in trouble and struggling in life.

****

Time soon flies when you have a focus. When you are clear enough on your WHY. And when you know you are creating something wonderful.

This is what happened for the two of us.

We continued to help at the homeless shelter, and we know we made a difference to at least those people's lives. It pushed us forward with our own plans though too.

A new place came along in 2018, by which time we had worked on our own businesses enough to have saved the money for a new start.

Not only was it a new start in terms of our home life, we had also been working on ourselves. My partner wasn't as excited as I was about self-development, but he was prepared to dip his toe in the water!

So, for our Valentine's Day treat to each other, we could have found ourselves in Paris, the City of Love. But no, we were watching a motivational speaker! Fair play to my partner, not only did he go with me, but he even accepted the one condition I'd set of us going together, which was that we had to sit separately during the seminars!

During the breakthrough process this was deep work. I wanted to gain as much as I could from being in the presence of other like-minded souls and inspirational experts. I wanted to focus on the positive energy from the others in the room. We needed to process our demons separately. And of course, if we were sitting together, surely this would create distractions!

I'm not sure he was as comfortable mixing with others in such a personal transformation at first. But, as the day went on, we both loved it. I was so caught up in the excitement of being there and in amongst this amazing high vibe environment, I almost forgot he had even gone with me!

And so, that was the real start of my new flight path, and the last time I would allow myself to be pushed to the side.

Chapter 14

Discovering My Wings

I said we had already started working on ourselves by the time we moved into our new home. I felt I was well on the way towards the real me finally being revealed.

Even this came with its surprising sideways turns though.

The thing is, when you know what you want and your desire for your destiny is unwavering, a strength can appear from nowhere. Is it strength? Is it commitment? I guess it's a combination of everything that your body and soul know they need to get you ready for take-off!

For me, I was no longer prepared to let little things get in the way.

I had already had a taste of what it would be like to be on the stage as a motivator and speaker when I was delivering business presentations all around the world, and I knew this was something I was destined for. I just didn't know how.

Sometimes, it's dwelling too long on the "how" that stops us from setting off on our journey. I didn't know it back then, but I didn't need to think about the how at all. Trusting in the opportunities being shown to me would have been enough!

So, for example, when the opportunity had arisen to attend the Public Speaker University event some time back, of course I jumped at the chance. You know by now that my nan never questioned my ability, and she offered to lend me the money to be there. I am so pleased she made it happen, because it propelled me forward in so many ways.

From then, signs appeared all over the place. Not always direct signals. But I was so driven on becoming something more, I kept going!

I was more ready, willing, and able to set off on this new path of self-development than my partner was, so when he received an email offering an even greater chance to become a 'crew member' for something I saw as huge events, he forwarded it on to me.

I was so determined to be there and be part of the team, I took every single opportunity and contacted the organisers by every single means possible, to get my name on that list. And it became my next massive step towards who I am now.

When you know something is so right, but blocks appear, you will find a way. So when another huge change to develop my speaking skills came up, I found myself sitting in the interview booth anyway. Despite all the old stuff that had been stuck in my head about not being good enough, and mum telling me I was lazy and would never make anything of myself, I heard myself saying to the guy interviewing me, "I can't afford to come into this academy right now. But I'm telling you now, I *will* be on the stage with Andy Harrington."

A phrase that I came across around that time was so appropriate to that moment, because he clearly had faith in me. He told me he knew I would be there, without doubt! So, I will say the same thing to you.

Even if you don't believe in yourself right now, borrow the belief from somebody else who does!

There are plenty of people around you who see more in you than you ever will. Remember me saying that my nan saw more in me than my mum and I ever saw? It's true. And that's something else I love about doing what I do. I get to step back and look at my coaching clients, trainee speakers and presenters, and all those who come into my community, with a different perspective. I can look at their potential, I can see their character, without the same pressure they load onto themselves.

The same goes for you. I see you, too, as the awesome person you are!

A lesson for us all, is that whilst it might have knocked me that the academy wasn't for me at that time, what I did do was step into the alternatives that arose.

I started to, what we call, "crew" for Andy. I got to attend the events, and be part of the team who helped out with the delegates. I could support and encourage the attendees, whilst learning at the same time.

Andy was one of a syndicate of inspirational and motivational speakers. So, not only did I get the opportunity to put myself forward for crewing at his events, I also got to do the same for the other syndicate members.

This was a whole new world for me. One I wished I had found out about years before.

But then maybe I wasn't ready for this any earlier. I still had a whole heap of learning to do—about myself, more than anything else—before I could step out with confidence to do what I do.

I recognised so much about myself—some of which I am pleased to acknowledge. Most of which I see needed to change. But that change could only come when I was ready for it to happen. Had I tried to fit in with what life was "supposed" to be? Had I tried to be like so many other people? Without doubt.

I see myself now in my videos, I hear myself on guest speaker slots, and on the stage, and I know my mum helped to get me here. My nan and grandad were pivotal. The partners I have spent time with have developed my character and resilience.

And I know now, I was always destined to be slightly different!

I was reminded of something I'd heard Andy say when I first saw him on the stage, and thought to myself,

"Why do you try so hard to fit in when you were born to stand out?"
- Andy Harrington

Whilst all of this was taking off for me, and my self-development game was levelling up at every turn, the business was booming too.

I mentioned that my partner and I had taken inspiration from our nans, and named the business after them - Jean Properties Ltd. Well, if we hadn't created that business and expanded on the original company structure, things would have been different.

My cleaning company was doing great. Together, we then developed the maintenance side of the business, which boomed! And finally, we reached the point where we could move into property, rental of serviced apartments.

The relationship itself has now taken on a solely business-based guise. But I have to say, it was so obviously meant to be.

I am eternally grateful for the additional business knowledge and determination that he brought to the partnership, combined with our joint devotion to making Jean Properties Limited a success.

In an earlier chapter, I mentioned that when nan allowed me to move back in with her, it was a favour that I didn't know at the time would be returned. Well, it was. And without the business named after her, I wouldn't have been able to step back from my professional life to care for her when she needed me.

I never realised how important it is to look to the future, plan ahead, and consider at least one Plan B. Perhaps that was my biggest part of growing up—really growing up—not being the pretend grown up cooking in the toy kitchen. Or the little girl cooking meals for herself when home alone.

For me, there was no Plan B, just a diversion that sometimes cannot be avoided. I have come to realise that when you are on the right path, and might face a slight reroute, nothing can stop you from veering back to your true flight path - your true destiny.

But the beauty of all of this is, now I know I had to go through everything to become who I am now.

Even the days when running my own events, I would often arrive at the venue to find out someone determined to ruin it for me had called to cancel it.

Yes, the fall of the advertising company left not just my own money and mindset in shatters, but also others who had followed me in. In fact, the "ripple effect" that I usually refer to in positive terms, had taken a negative turn, and the bitterness and blame were coming at me from all angles. As I had become so well-known within the company, those outside of my immediate circle of team members and downline also decided to join the pity parade and aim their revenge streaks in my direction. I totally understand that they wanted someone to blame, and I was the closest they could get to.

160

I steered clear of social media for around two years. I kept my new location and my plans to myself. But still they managed to track me down.

It got to a point where I had to create passwords for venue staff, so if anyone called to make any changes to my plans or requirements, they wouldn't alter anything without the "secret code," which only I knew.

They tried their hardest to bring me down, but the events all took place, and I even took photos and live videos to prove it! My messages came across so clearly that through the toughest of times, the community you hold dear and close to you will help you rise.

I can joke about it now, but if only they had used their innovation and detective skills positively, I would love some of those characters on my team right now! Resilience, fortitude, adaptability, and so much more came into play. And it has all helped me.

I have learned so much. And I am blessed to have been welcomed into the circles of many other motivational people, too, who not only teach me and mentor me, but also make time for me. In fact, one of these special people has written the foreword in this book.

Others who have come and gone, were here for as long as they needed to be.

The behaviours I was shown have taught me valuable lessons.

Lessons that have enabled me to create my personal values of trust, freedom, loyalty, and, above all, honesty. Values that have also been incorporated within my company and in the lessons I now also coach my clients.

They say, "When the student is ready, the teacher will appear." Well, it has certainly been true for me. My time eventually came to **grow**.

I realised that everything was in fact not happening *to* me, but *for* me. And I hope that you, too, will feel that same amazing feeling.

It truly is an enlightening moment when you realise that everything in life is exactly how it is meant to be.

I said that this book is not just to tell you my story, but to give guidance and recommendations too.

And this is where the next part begins.

My Lessons, My Learnings, and My Message to You

My reason for finally writing this book, and so openly sharing my story, is so you, too, can learn from my vast array of detours and diversions off what I'd hoped would be a straightforward flightpath to finding my destiny!

Not necessarily to help you avoid getting into any similar, let's say "dubious" relationships or business partnerships. But more to remind you to use whatever the outcome is positively, as something to learn from.

Some relationships and partnerships turn out to be exactly what we need. You know the type of people you should be spending your time with, in that case.

If you're lucky enough to be in business with someone who is on the same page as you, and you each get to use your skills to the best advantage and greater good for your business and customers, you're already on your way to winning at life!

Others, though, will go "POP" on us!

And that's life, as my nan would say.

There is no handbook that comes with you as you enter this world. You will pick up bits and pieces along the way. But one of the biggest lessons you can learn is to try to find a positive in every situation.

That doesn't mean you get the toxic positivity label. The one who, no matter what, acts like they always come up smelling of roses with a Cheshire Cat grin. It simply means you will be able to view life through a different lens.

The relationships that go pop will, undoubtedly, teach you invaluable lessons about the other person or people involved. But look closer to home, and they will actually, more importantly, teach you invaluable lessons about you.

You might not see the learnings right away. So you'll probably go feet first straight back into the same or similar circumstances again, and again until you do. I'm not generalising here by the way, this is a fact! People say they attract karma as if it's always a bad thing. Karma isn't a punishment or revenge. It actually means lessons to be learned, and until we learn those lessons, things will continue to remain the same.

For instance, have you ever wondered why you seem to attract the same kind of characters, friends, partners into your life? Why you go through what feels like a never-ending chain of problems or misfortunes? Does it feel as though your life is a story waiting to be written (a drama, or a comedy, in some cases!)

Think back to my own stories. I was repeatedly attracting the kind of guys who were financially unstable, needed help in some way or another, and were totally unreliable. I was constantly putting up with things I shouldn't have tolerated, which I know now was a result of my lack of self-worth. And where did that come from? The example of being told the ballet school had closed down, simply because mum didn't think I was good enough to go. Was I an embarrassment to her? Had she genuinely been told I wasn't good enough? Or was I just not good enough in her eyes? Was it even anything to do with me not being good enough? Whatever the reason, this limiting belief had been instilled in me before the age of seven - remember, that crucial and pivotal period of our lives.

It is no coincidence, then, that this went on until I started working on ME. I don't believe that anything is a coincidence in life. The Universe has its own way of letting us know what's what.

But do we always listen to our intuition, or notice the signs?

I studied. I was open to facing awkward aha moments. I unravelled a lifetime, up until that point, of being pushed to the side, abandoned, getting into debt and struggling to bring myself back on a firm financial footing, losing my home, and everything else you have read about in this book. So, as I knew no different, and thought that was the way life was, I accepted it and almost beckoned it into my world from the outside too.

When you finally "get it" and understand what the message is that you have to learn. When you have come to a point where you can take no more of being treated that way (or *allowing* yourself to be treated that way). When your desire to move away from this never-ending cycle is eventually greater than the comfort of staying where you are. *Then*, you have learned your lesson.

And once you acknowledge and accept that lesson, you are ready to follow the new path ahead.

I was definitely living in the "effect" side and not the "cause." I refer to each of these with my clients, as it is a very hard, yet extremely important, lesson to learn. Through the power of these reference points, we achieve a whole new perspective, a massive eye-opener, on how they look at and approach situations.

When you start to grasp the concept of cause and effect in life, you'll also start to notice that the people you attract are more aligned to you, your goals, your values, and are worthy of being in your world. You no longer have to feel good enough to be invited into theirs.

So, this is the first in a list of the many lessons I learned whilst rediscovering my inner strength, my power, and my destiny.

I have not written them in order of their importance, because none of us are the same. Each chapter and lesson learned will resonate with your own circumstances differently. The lessons and messages coming out of them are listed simply from the connections that came up for me as I was writing each chapter. They are what has also helped me define my presentations and coaching programmes.

Like I said, I have gone through all of this to make some sense of it all for you! And this is how it all works.

Emotional Foundationing

I'm still using everything my grandparents taught me, to project onto other people's lives, your lives, and help you create firm foundations to building an amazing life. It also involves cutting through the crap that we have lived with, the conditioned thoughts and beliefs, and replacing it with far better footings.

It's what I call Emotional Foundationing (a Corinna-ism, by the way. You won't find it on Google).

Some of you may think I've got confused with Emotional Intelligence, but no, this is completely different in my world.

Emotional Foundationing for me is all about:

1) Focusing on what you want;
2) Understanding your WHY; and
3) Not putting all your eggs in one basket.

When I created the concept of Emotional Foundationing, I was so clear on what I wanted, I had no doubts whatsoever that it was going to be successful, and it was the way forward for me.

Nan might just say if you want to run a business then it's plain and simple common sense that these are the things you focus on. But that was years back when there were fewer external distractions, no social media pressure, and comparison-itis wouldn't have even been afforded a sideways glance.

It was also way back before mindset, mental health awareness, and personal development were thought of, let alone considered crucial factors within the personal or professional world.

So, let's break them down.

Knowing where you are right now, and what you want or where you want to get to, might sound like an obvious place to start.

In truth though, it's often what stops people with a vague business idea, or a hope to create a better life or become a better person, from even taking the first step towards their goals.

It's not surprising that many of my clients come to me for one thing, and realise that it's actually not that thing that's holding them back or stopping them from making a clear goal, and therefore not achieving it!

Sometimes it's easier to work out what you definitely DON'T want first. It's all part of the wonders of the mind – reverse engineering and reverse psychology.

Psychology is a fascinating thing. I have spent hundreds of hours studying the mind, how it impacts us (positively and negatively), and what we can do to change our mindset.

As you know, all of this has come from the experiences I have had, and the need to bring about a change in my life.

So whilst you are reading through the following sections, try to consider how you, too, could introduce some of these aspects into your life.

Mindset, Motivation and Mental Clarity

I would like to point out right from the outset that I am not a Business Coach. I can help you in many aspects of running a business, but do not expect me to coach you in systems, processes, policies, and legalities.

What I know for sure, though, is that one of the most fundamental things for any business owner, no matter what type of business, is **mindset**.

The same goes for you whether you are a business owner, entrepreneur, employee, or simply want to improve your life and get out of the rut you have fallen into.

I mentioned earlier about being able to find the positives in every situation. Of course, you cannot even expect to see positives through difficult circumstances, or unexpected negative situations, if your mindset is in the wrong place.

In order to understand your mindset, you must be prepared to start with the inner work.

This involves not only the uncoiling of many years of conditioning, along with flattening a mountain of limiting beliefs, negative self-talk, and unsavoury behaviours. But it also then leads on to the next steps – the improvements, if you like – and taking inspired action to get to where you want to be.

One of my biggest shifts was changing my mindset from that "woe is me" victim mentality, to the realisation of things happening *for* me and not *to* me.

In fact, now I truly believe my life has changed and my destiny awaits because things are happening *because* of me!

So how did my mindset change? And how can you hope to achieve a turnaround of your mindset? I mean, I am guessing you have got this far through the book because you *want* to make changes, right?!

It's not a case of waking up one morning and telling your old inner voices to go and do one!!

It takes time, effort, patience, and understanding.

You can do it on your own if you wish. But it's far easier when you have at least one other person with you to be your cheerleader, to remind you of the progress you have made, and continue to make. And to keep you accountable for every inspired action you have on your tasks.

Someone who has been where you are now, and understands what it takes to put yourself in the vulnerable position of letting go. I'll talk more about accountability later.

The benefits of achieving this mindset shift though are beyond brilliant!

From a personal perspective, you can be assured that you are not going back down those same one-way streets, stuck in a one way relationship, where everything is give, give, give, only to receive nothing in return. At least nothing that serves you any purpose.

You will sense a new-found confidence to put personal boundaries in place. Boundaries that will protect you, keep safe space for you, and will eventually benefit those around you too.

Remember to communicate these new boundaries though, otherwise you will be faced with a raft of moans and groans and misunderstandings when your behaviours and reactions suddenly change!

As for business benefits?

Wow! When your mindset shifts, and you allow yourself to open up to new opportunities, reach the mental clarity around where you are right now, clarity around your WHY, and you become crystal clear about what you want to achieve, then the world becomes your oyster, (or lobster) too.

The first hurdle many entrepreneurs come up against is that they never quite pin down what success looks like for them.

Do you remember way back at the beginning of this book, I referred to the need to work out what is success for you? What does it look like? What will it feel like? How will life be when you have achieved success? Or how will you even know when you get there? This is my point.

Without knowing your goals and your vision, knowing your version of success, what will bring you happiness and fulfilment – personally and professionally - how can you expect to reach your destiny?

Only when I had studied this myself in great detail, and I knew what my purpose and my WHY actually were, could I start to focus on my business. I'll also come back to my WHY shortly.

What about you though? What will you start with? Have you worked out your WHY? Do you know what success is for you?

Have you thought about why you are reading this book, and want to make your world a better place? Are you doing it for other people around you? Or can you, hand on heart say, it is primarily for you?

The great thing about doing any inner work, personal development, and making time for self-care of any kind, is that it has this flippin' amazing "ripple effect."

When you start to see, feel, and BE the benefits of the hard work (and it is hard work, by the way, you have to be prepared for that), you will see those around you start to feel the benefits too.

Coming back to business though and how I learned the lessons. Despite losing an awful lot of money over a short time period, I took it in my stride. Of course, I was pretty peeved at the time, as you can probably tell from my version of events.

I said I had to step back from social media for a while after the MLM balloon had burst. That was my time to regroup. To look at what was actually achievable. Yes, the main income stream had gone, but what had I been able to do whilst it was still flying high?

I'd grown massively as a person. I started speaking on stage—can you imagine Miss H seeing me up there? My self-esteem and confidence reached a level I had never experienced, and continue to soar. I was already coaching others in how to set up their starter businesses, and how to manage their customers.

The fact that the guy at the top pulled the rug from under us doesn't detract from the fact that these people had been successful in what they were doing. And I learned enough about the business itself to be able to sell it to others.

What came out of that particular situation is an amazing resilience and fortitude.

I look back now and recognise how much I learned during the process about managing business effectively and efficiently. I became a bit of a pro in debt management, tax, and financial accounting, which obviously helped my cleaning business too. I had put a lot on the line when I sold my house to fund my first business. I wouldn't recommend that without seeking professional financial advice first. And I won't be doing it again myself without the same!

Every step of every path I took back then was worth it. And that's a completely different mindset.

I had been living in a so-called 'Poor Mindset' of constantly complaining when things went wrong, but was never brave enough to take that final step to owning a business myself. I was afraid of missing out.

Shiny Object Syndrome struck more than one chord with me, I practically had a symphony! I would let myself get so far into something, start doing well with it, and then get distracted by the next thing coming along.

What I needed to do, and eventually did, was to change my perspective, and start thinking the way of a 'Rich Mindset' business owner.

- I kicked all the bad habits from my past.
- I acknowledged the mistakes I'd made, and learned from them.
- I found that being open minded helped me over, under, around and through various hurdles along the way.
- I started to put myself first.

Taking better care of me helped massively towards coming off the medication, gaining so much more clarity, and being willing to see things from a different perspective.

I guess I had always been on the lookout for the next thing that would make me a fast buck as well. Or maybe even a glimpse into the world of the wheeler-dealers I'd seen on the markets where I'd spent so long with grandad.

Ironically, it was the MLM business that taught me nothing is ever a quick win!

It wasn't just me though. I know hundreds of people who enter the world of network marketing thinking it's going to be easy. There's generally a brand that you can fall back on to boost your publicity. The systems are already set up. More often than not, there are social media posts you can even copy and paste.

At first glance, it seems like all the hard work is done. Remember if something seems too good to be true, it usually is!

What they don't always tell you though is that people still buy YOU! Your customers want to see YOU.
Yes, you can sit behind a well-known, or super exciting novel and new name, but you still have to do some work yourself.

If you don't go into it with the right mindset – remember, this is a business, not a hobby (although it can be, if you're not wanting to make a full-time income from it) - then the reality is, you won't get to where you want to be, I'm afraid.

If you consider any business a side-hustle, a side-hustle is how it will always remain.

I am pointing this out to you from experience. Already £20k in debt, I then lost a whole heap more.

Was I prepared for that? Had I set myself up thinking I needed a Plan B? No!

There I was, flying high on buzz from being on stage, from sharing this "great business opportunity" with others. I didn't even consider what might happen if for any reason this income came to an end.

Personally, I was like a completely different person. My reliance on other people, and external validation, was slowly disappearing. Is this something you resonate with? Do you feel stuck in a cycle of not just wanting someone around you, but *needing* them there? It's not a great place to be, I can tell you. And it was a huge relief to finally start feeling free of it all.

Some of the change came as a result of the medication, there is no doubt. I will say here that my view around taking tablets simply to ease the pain and numb the feeling remains the same. It is the *root cause* that needs to be worked on, not just the symptom.

Only when I eased back on the medication did I find the mental clarity I needed to have, in order to move forwards. But it was the questions I asked myself that gave me the motivation and then inspiration to get started on the route I have now taken.

Which reminds me, if you are wondering how a change in mindset could help you in other ways, consider also your finances – personal or professional.

Money Mindset

The fact that I kept finding these guys who were not on stable financial footings, and almost always ended up owing me money, says just as much about me and my money mindset as it did about theirs.

It was the whole thing about 'like attracting like'. Only I didn't see it like that, did I? I blamed them all the time for getting themselves in a mess, and me *having* to lend them money. So it was then their fault that I ended up in debt too.

But, when I looked inwardly and took away any of the blame, things started to improve.

I'd seen a change when I was working hard in the cleaning business, and mixing with the entrepreneurs of a different mindset, so I knew it could work. I knew I didn't want the lavish lifestyle, but I also knew I started to feel better about myself when I was surrounded by luxury and nice things.

So, when I found something I genuinely wanted to do (the first step in Emotional Foundationing), I got clear on my WHY (step two), and started to see the life changes I was helping create in my clients, it was the cherry on the cake.

My money mindset had also shifted massively by that time.

I no longer blamed anyone else, or even myself. I could see the difference between working long hours to get things done and through urgent need for money, versus being more efficient in a shorter time. I started to take responsibility and ownership for myself and everything that was showing up for me, and because of me.

And, check this out for a mindset shift, instead of worrying and moaning about the amount of tax I pay now, I see it as a blessing!

Yes, how does that sit with you?

The mere fact you have a tax bill proves that you are earning sufficient as an employee, or making money in your business as an entrepreneur. Do you see what I mean? Find the positive!

I said I was coming back to my WHY. It's what helps me to see the silver lining with every cloud.

What Is My WHY?
What keeps you going when business gets hard, you lose motivation, you've just had enough, or you can't be bothered one day?

What ignites that fire within you again?

Maybe that fire has already burned out, and all you're left with is the embers?

Well, let's get it back, and get you "fired up to face the world!"

My nan and grandad passed down so much knowledge, character, and charisma, which is also a part of Emotional Foundationing in business and life.

Nan said she sometimes felt as though she had failed her own children, so I guess she would have said she had failed with her WHY.

What she didn't see when she was telling me that, was that she had everything inside of her to live an amazing life, and teach me that way too.

My nan's legacy will not only be the clothes and jewellery of hers that I still wear. But so much more.

She taught me the best way to succeed is to be the best version of yourself. If you are honest, authentic, and want to see others do well then why would you not attract the right people into your life?

Nan and grandad have always been my WHY, not just the two of them personally, but everything they taught me. And I am now passing on to others, such as you.

Jean Properties Limited, which if you remember is the property company my partner and I established in honour of our nans, was actually a saving grace. Ironically, with my nan being half of my WHY, it was this business that enabled me to take time out to care for her when she needed it.

Nan and grandad will always be my WHY.

When I became clear on this, my motivation was there immediately.

NOTES

What does success look like for you?

How will you know when you have achieved success or reached your destiny?

What is your WHY?

What kind of mindset do you operate in?

What could you improve?

Motivation

I didn't wait for, or need, any further motivation than to make my nan and grandad proud.

I will say this to you though, DO NOT wait for motivation to strike.

Another key factor, particularly if you are in business or looking to start up a new business, is that motivation doesn't come from success. Success comes from having had the motivation in the first place to get up from your seat, putting yourself out there in all weathers, under all circumstances, and despite all distractions. So, you have to have the motivation to drive you to success and onwards to find your destiny.

Think of it like riding a bike.

The pedals don't simply start to move just because you *thought about* going for a bike ride. You have to have the motivation to get on the bike, to put your foot on the pedal, and to push away, forcing the pedals to move and the wheels to turn.

Motivation comes before motion. But before you have the motivation, you do need the clarity on what you want to achieve!

Do you see how all of this is interlinked?

They all come together as a package.

The more mental clarity we have before we even start a new business, the more creative we also become.

I thought I was clear when I was working all the hours *in* the cleaning business. And working on my own and other business websites. And pet sitting, too. I'm exhausted just thinking about it now.

I wasn't clear at all. I wasn't driven by motivation. I was driven by desperation.

Operating from a place of lack and fear of failing leaves you in a negative state.

You find yourself surrounded by negative vibes. And reaching out for anything and everything to get you through.

These are the times when you will attract the wrong situations, people, and experiences.

Was it because I didn't think I was good enough at one single thing, so wanted to give myself a way out?

Did I have doubts in myself and my own abilities?

Had this come from mum saying I would never make anything of myself?

Possibly all of the above.

I even had doubts as to whether I was good enough to crew for Andy's events. Was the fact that my partner had received the email and not me a sign that I wasn't good enough for them to take on? I wasn't capable of doing the job?

This was after I'd already been working on 'me' for months.

That's what I mean when I say each time we step up to another level or another challenge, those pesky inner voices are likely to return.

But what did I do then? Did I let the inner voices and 'conditioning' stop me? No!

I took the bull by the bloody horns and went and did it anyway.

You can read more about my thoughts on facing fear in my eBook "The Art of Feeling Fear and Taking Back Control."

Working with Andy was an opportunity I was NOT going to let my fear get in the way of.

And I am so pleased I gave my inner voice a good talking to, because being part of the crew opened up doors to so many more opportunities.

Anyway, back to the many businesses I was running.

Now, don't get me wrong. Even Warren Buffett advocates having more than one source of income, and with a $97 billion net worth at the time of writing, who am I to argue with him?!

I do agree with multiple income streams. Just not at the expense of your health, relationships, and mental wellbeing. Or because you don't trust in yourself to succeed at any one of them alone.

NOTES

What motivates you?

What do you enjoy doing?

Who inspires you?

How do they inspire you?

Don't Put All your Eggs in One Basket

If you want to start another business or diversify, and feel totally aligned to doing it, one thing I would strongly recommend is being comfortable and confident in your original business before stepping into another.

I briefly mentioned one element of my mindset shift has been taking ownership and responsibility for my actions.

Accepting anything that hasn't worked out as I wanted it to or expected it to, is now a valuable lesson, not a waste of time, money, or effort.

Even when it's hard, things have gone wrong, and you could just give up, true authenticity is all about remembering why you're doing what you do.

Successful business owners, and individuals who are happy and fulfilled, learn to appreciate the lessons learned in life. I no longer see anything that's gone awry, or off course, as a fail.

I believe we actually learn more from the lessons when things don't quite fall into place.

Serena Williams is a great advocate of lessons learned from losses.

"I don't like to lose at anything ... Yet I've grown most not from victories, but setbacks. If winning is God's reward, then losing is how he teaches us."

Similarly, I would urge you to take accountability for whatever decisions you make.

You may lose money, pride, or reputation. I have come through all of those, and I'm still here to tell you the tale.

My partner and I could have gone back to that pity party we invited ourselves to after we lost the house, and things had to change. We had to accept responsibility for ourselves and our own fate. We had to become accountable for our own actions and attitudes. I'm not quite sure who we thought we were, or why we believed the world owed us a favour, but my god, did we need to grow up!

"When you forgive, you heal. And when you let go, you grow."

In the process of self-discovery and moving forward, we sometimes lose people along the way.

It's the acknowledgement that their journey is just not yours, and letting them go, that creates the freedom to move on.

This is what has helped me to now be able to talk more openly about my life, and let go of the emotional attachment and meaning I'd given to each experience.

This leads nicely to my next point.

Attitude

I've talked about mindset already, and attitude could be included within that. However, I really want to talk more here about having an open mind.

Life changes and becomes so much calmer once you allow yourself to be open to more opportunities, signs, and signals.

Now, I consider signs related to situations as a great teacher, too.

Not the kind of teacher who stands you up in front of the class when you've asked for help, as a tiny child, and fills you with the dread of ever being seen or heard again.

Just a subtle lesson dotted here and there during our days, telling us something needs to change, or we should start taking more notice of something specific.

I learned this myself and can 100% vouch for the fact that it does happen.

Trusting Your Gut Instinct

I mentioned in a few chapters that I have learned to trust, and that I generally follow, my gut instinct.

You may laugh and wonder how on earth I could have possibly gone through everything I did if my gut instinct was so connected!

Truth is, I wish I'd learned about the power of the mind/body connection years ago. It could have saved me no end of heartache, and an absolute fortune!

I didn't really know too much about what that sickly feeling (the one I tend to get in my chest rather than my stomach) was trying to tell me. I just knew I felt sick, and maybe I had to be careful.

I possibly (subconsciously) avoided listening to it, or tried to prove it wrong (not a good move, by the way). I certainly didn't know about it, or take any notice of it, when I went full-on into Multi-Level Marketing!

Now though, with the knowledge and experience that I have built through personally using, and coaching with, NLP and ECT (Neuro-Linguistic Programming and Emotional Change Therapy), I know more about how our minds work, and what they help us to do or can stop us from achieving.

Our gut feel can work just as well for business as it can for personal circumstances.

1. I have learned what questions to ask – is this feeling telling me I shouldn't be getting into this relationship/business partnership because I'm scared of it? Or is it telling me it's not the right person/plan? When you start to use the "five whys" (like a child constantly asking "why?" with each response they receive) you can start delving deep into your answer.

    The beauty of learning about how the mind and body work together is that you start to recognise signals, signs, and symptoms as soon as they pop up. So you are able to do something about it.

2. I have learned when to follow my body rather than my brain – remember, the human brain

tries to control everything for us. But the body is always right.

My good friend and mentor, Jessen James, recommends making decisions first from the heart (i.e. the body) before then referring back to the mind.

Your body can tell you to push forward with something, you're all fired up and ready to do it, until .... that pesky inner voice, aka the mind, tells you to stop!

That's when the reminder and recollection of past experiences strikes. Doubt creeps in. Imposter Syndrome (if that is even a thing) pops up. And suddenly, your head is back in control, and stops you in your tracks. So what can you do about it? Again, ask the "five whys" if you need to, refer to other methods of checking in with the body (sway testing and muscle testing are a couple of the more well-known methods). Another inspiration for me is Mel Robbins. Her 'Five Second Rule' is great. It works on the premise that you have five seconds from first thinking about doing something i.e. getting out of bed on the alarm, going for a run, before your brain (and mind monkeys) steps in to tell you "no." So, when I was working on overcoming my OCD, I thought about how I could get out of my usual habitual behaviours, and did the new step before my brain could talk me out of it. For instance, I would get in the car and put my hands on the steering wheel within that five second gap, before my brain told me I had to wipe my hands. Or I'd sit down to eat my sandwiches, and open them up within that same gap, before I went into panic mode about my hands being dirty.

Go on, try it! See how much more productive you can be if you take action as soon as you think about doing something, before you talk yourself out of it. Please make sure it is safe and sensible though. I take no responsibility for random acts of daftness, just because you did it within five seconds!

3. I have learned to acknowledge, and accept, that the answer I receive might not always be the one I *want* to hear, but it is the right answer for that situation at that time. Even if things don't come to you when you want them to, or how you expect them to be delivered, the Universe always delivers what and how it is meant to do for your destiny to unfold.

When I talk about taking notice of signs and signals, and then taking the necessary actions to follow them up, I often use a specific scenario to explain it. Something you will all be familiar with.

You don't just think about ordering something online and then expect it to be delivered. You have to take the inspired action, follow up on your intention. You deliberately choose the item, choose the supplier, place the order, pay for it and then you can sit back and expect it to be delivered.

In the same way with personal or professional life – you can't just imagine life is going to be wonderful, you are going to achieve success (and because you've followed my guidance earlier, you now know what success means, looks like and feels like for you!) and then expect it to happen. You have to take that intended and inspired action to make sure you get there.

Basically though, if signs, events, experiences appear, don't ignore them. Just because they might not seem relevant at that time, let them sit in your subconscious, comfortably in the back of your mind. When the same signs, events or experiences are given to you again, maybe it's the Universe now telling you to take note and to take action.

NOTES

How and when does intuition and/or gut feel show up for you?

Do you recognise your gut instinct? What do you do when you sense it?

Do you recall a time when your gut instinct was called upon? How did it serve you? Was it right?

When have you received signs or signals that you have deliberately chosen to ignore?

What was the outcome/lesson learned? Do you wish you had taken notice?

Setting Goals

When you know what you want in life, when you are clear on where you want to go, in life or in business, that's the time to be aware of your budget! Do the maths! The calculations are crucial.

You have probably giggled your way through my financial losses – I would!

You also know I went into the MLM world hoping it to be the last thing I would have to do in order to reach millionaire status and for my grandparents to be proud of me. The first millionaire in the family. Imagine that! Well, I did.

Be crystal clear on what each next step is going to be, what it's going to cost, what you need to know, and what you need to do.

And how do you do this?

Reverse Engineer. Start at the end, with your end goal in sight, and work backwards.

I often refer my clients to the concept of 'set it and forget it,' which might sound counter-intuitive, but it makes sense.

Think about it, how many goals have you focused on and not achieved? How many goals have you set, not had a plan in place, and yet still achieved?

When the goal is set, consistent actions are required. BUT ... allowing yourself to let go of the attachment to the outcome, the attachment of achieving it, relieves the pressure you could be over-burdening yourself with.

Similar to the suggestion I made earlier about how working out what you *don't* want helps you to decipher what you *do* want!

Working your steps out in reverse makes sure you don't miss a step. You HAVE to think what comes next if you're doing it backwards. It works when you are working on process flows too, to make sure you have included each customer touch point, for instance.

Have you ever tried saying the alphabet the wrong way round? It takes a lot more time and effort to think about what letter comes next. And you're less likely to get it wrong by doing it this way.

Be Creative

If you're open to taking on board signs and signals from the Universe, and reverse engineering your success, then I'm sure you're up for using your creativity too!

Allow your thoughts to be free.

It's sod's law that your best thoughts will always come to you at the most inopportune moments. Like when you pay a visit to the bathroom.

What would I recommend?

Keep your phone with you and make notes in the app. Keep a note pad next to your bed.

Also, be prepared for your thoughts and creativity to come up when you are focused on something else.

You can sit at your desk for hours, and still not have managed to create a single social media post or a slide for a presentation.

Go somewhere else and focus on something else, and you'll become your most creative.

1. Get outside for a walk, or at least a breath of fresh air.
2. Hang the washing out.
3. Take the dogs for a wander.
4. Put on some high-vibe upbeat music to raise your energy levels.
5. Meditate.
6. Listen to an inspirational podcast.
7. Make that call to a friend you've been putting off for ages.
8. Have a coffee or, better still, drink some water or herbal tea.
9. Anything that doesn't need your full attention, and allows your mind to relax.

If you're still struggling come the end of the day, have a bath and an early night.

Journal before bed though. Get everything from inside your head down on paper. And you will be surprised how much your unconscious mind processes overnight.

It always works for me. In fact, even if I have had some great ideas and I need to mull them over, I can guarantee that next morning I will have come up with something that's 10 times better than what I thought of before.

The power of the unconscious mind is phenomenal. Just trust the process.

I often stop and think *"what would nan say? What would her gran before her say?"*

These are the moments that I could really do with taking a step back and refocusing. And I highly recommend any of the above if you find yourself in a similar position.

A final recommendation is to keep a journal or notebook of some sort next to your bed. I know it's taking steps back considering you could use your phone, but I honestly think physically handwriting on real paper adds to the process of clearing the mind.

There are times of course when you will have thoughts and can't easily write them down, so I also have a Dictaphone in the car - I know! Even more of a step back in time!! (Whatever you do when you are driving, please stay safe and legal).

NOTES

Now is a great time to start thinking about your goals. Do you know what you want?

If you don't yet know what you do want, do you know what you don't want?

What is your vision? Where do you see yourself 3, 5, 10 years from now?

How are you going to get there?

What's stopping you, if anything?

What would help you achieve your goals?

To round up, I said throughout "Wings of Destiny", and the learnings I share with you, you will learn:

- ✔ How to change the outcome of your situation by thinking differently.
- ✔ How your own words, in your head and spoken, have a huge impact on your results in life.
- ✔ How I turned my own heartache and pain into *your* new power.
- ✔ How to feel happier and less stressed.
- ✔ How to live with passion and purpose every day.

So, what have you learned?

1. How to change the outcome of your situation by thinking differently

Peeling away the layers of the onion of your life, being open to inner work, and changing your mindset are all fundamental within personal development. Particularly if you want to improve your life, step up in your business, and think differently about life.

You have read about my own experiences of rediscovering my inner strength, power, and finding my destiny.

How much are you prepared to do?

It would be great to see you joining my community through social media, join me at an event if I'm in your area, or arrange a Discovery Call to chat about my coaching programmes. You will be able to bring all of this and more into your world.

What can you do now to change your mindset and think differently?

2. How your own words, in your head and spoken, have a huge impact on your results in life
Take a moment to consider your own inner voice, mind monkeys, and conditioned negative beliefs. Where do you think they came from?

Who supports you? Who do you allow to impact your thoughts today?

What do you catch yourself saying? Do you take any notice?

What do your words and your language stop you from doing?

How could life be if you could silence your inner voice and quieten your inner critic?

3. How I turned my own heartache and pain into *your* new power

Well, I think I've probably told you enough about my story so far.

You've read the detail (what was appropriate to print, at least!) and have seen how I have reframed my past perspective. How I used personal development to turn my experiences into lessons. And how I now recognise that, without the life I have had, I most certainly wouldn't be here now.

Through my own work, and that which I have continued to learn so I can share with my clients, I have become an expert in the "reframe."

I've even learned to reframe that Black Box. I no longer see it linked to the deep, dark depression I went through. I now consider it a box of learning and light. A bright red box of information, intuition, and inspiration from all I have learned since the diagnosis and right back to my childhood in fact.

Take a few moments to write down what you have taken from my story and from the lessons learned.

4. How to feel happier and less stressed

That's easy. Pull together a combination of everything you have read so far!

No, seriously, it's amazing how uncomplicated life becomes when you:

A) remove yourself from negativity and toxic people, relationships and situations that no longer serve you;

B) learn how to disassociate the meanings and emotional attachments you have tied to your past, and allow yourself to move on;

C) take the pressure of external validation and expectation out of your life, live your life on your terms, and stop comparing yourself or your business to anyone else; and

D) can recognise what you are capable of, uncover your potential, and start to believe in yourself.

And that's just the start.

What can you do, starting today, to make your life happier and feel less stressed?

5. **How to live with passion and purpose every day**
    - Get crystal clear on what you want
    - Work out your WHY
    - Design a life and a business that are aligned to your values, goals, and ethics. A life you don't feel you need to escape from. A business from which you don't feel you need a distraction. Somewhere you feel you are at home and can be the best version of you.

Once you have all of the above in place, you will notice the change.

Let your business be your passion.

Aligning yourself with your business is not you going to a job, earning the money for someone else. Your heart has to be in your business, even though you might not be feeling it one day, or might have lost sight of your original vision.

My cleaning business was my first business and has always been my baby. It gave me back some of the self-esteem I had pushed out of my own body. It opened the door to personal development. In a roundabout way, it was the pathway to public speaking. And ultimately, I learned so much about what to do and what not to do in business from that first experience.

Without that business, which I hardly ever need to go into anymore, I wouldn't be where I am now.

I'll ask you again, what can you do today that will create a life of passion and purpose?

One Final Note

Remember, I have made my past mistakes so you might not have to!!

I said I wasn't a business coach, but what I will tell you is, ironically, the kind of information you probably already know.

The juicy nuggets you have probably watched in Facebook ads, and read in other coaches' email sequences, but simply not listened to.

My question is, why did you not take any notice?
Are you ready to listen now?

Because another thing I will tell you, is that if you do, if you listen to all the juicy nuggets that lay the foundation for an amazing future, encourage you to take the inspired action, and then you accept a level of accountability, you and your business will sky-rocket!

You see, what happens when you hear juicy nuggets of information over and over. And ignore them over and over. The brain thinks *"oh, so you're not interested then? OKAY, let's delete it, and anything like it in future. Tell you what, I'll fill your head with other stuff that's going to do you no good, but you took notice of it a hundred times before!"*

And what happens then?

You get so far in life and in business, and then those huge blocks appear. The ones that I referred to as reasons (that are actually excuses).

How much money and opportunity have you let pass you by so far?

I will help get you through those blocks so you can go and make the money that you deserve, and yet stays just out of reach. Or help build the confidence in you to stand up on the stage that has so far been your Nemesis. Or even just start to take the steps you've been avoiding.

Once you work out what you want, align with your WHY, and reach out for the help and guidance you might have been missing, you too will find your destiny. And I will be honoured to be right there alongside you when you're ready to take off.

I saw these beautiful words from the incomparable Donna Ashworth just as I was coming to the end of writing this book, and was drawn to share them with you, as I know they will serve at least one or two of you.

"If your mother did not love you ….

You owe it to that little girl to learn,
You owe it to her to make love,
You owe it to her to create a world so full of love, that it will eventually out-shadow the demons of your past …"

"Believe in your wings, and fly."

About the Author

Currently working on her passion educating entrepreneurs to reconnect and re-align with their business within a safe and supportive environment. Corinna resides in Essex, UK as an entrepreneur, Business & Life Alignment Coach, Multi Award Winning International Speaker, Hypnosis & Neuro-Linguistic Programming (NLP) Practitioner, Emotional Change Therapist (ECT), Investor & Author

After experiencing challenges in her own life and business, she soon released that many other established business owners and start-up business owners were experiencing similar problems...

Too much to do and too little time, overwhelmed, stress, money worries, whom to trust, relationship breakdowns and so on...

The one thing that kept her going was remembering her WHY and never letting go of her passion to help others.

After breaking through her own challenges and facing some life changing experiences, she realised the power of her own mind and by implementing strategies, she learned, adjusted, and adapted in how to deal with her emotions in a more powerful way, setting the foundations for her success. Now she helps other entrepreneurs and business owners reconnect with their inner power, removing blocks which are holding them back in their business and in life, supporting and educating so they can continue to achieve greatness even during challenging times.

Prior to starting her coaching and speaking journey she was working in travel for 20 years including 8 years as air cabin crew.

Corinna would love to serve you and believes that in both business and in life, we all have the ability to believe in our wings and fly!

Find out more at:

https://www.corinnastringer.co.uk/
https://www.facebook.com/CorinnaStringerOfficial
https://www.instagram.com/corinnastringerofficial/
https://www.linkedin.com/in/corinnastringerofficial/

Printed in Great Britain
by Amazon

17261633R00132